CONVERSATIONS
with my
DAD

Accessing your full potential by making the right choices at the right time.

Donald Middleton

Conversations with my Dad
Accessing Your Full Potential by Making the Right Choices at the Right Time.

Copyright © 2016 Donald Middleton

The views expressed by the author in reference to specific people in their book represent entirely their own individual opinions and are not in any way reflective of the views of Transformation Books. We assume no responsibility for errors, omissions or contradictory interpretation of the subject matter herein.

Transformation Books does not warrant the performance, effectiveness, or applicability of any websites listed in or linked to this publication. The purchaser or reader of this publication assumes responsibility of the use of these materials and information. Transformation Books shall in no event be held liable to any party for any direct, indirect, punitive, special, incidental, or any other consequential damages arising directly or indirectly from any use of this material. Techniques and processes given in this book are not to be used in place of medical or other professional advice.

No part of this book may be reproduced or transmitted in any form, or by any means, electronic or mechanical, including photography, recording, or in any information storage or retrieval system without written permission from the author or publisher, except in the case of brief quotations embodied in articles and reviews. If you are seeking permission, please email info@transformationbooks.com.

Published by:
Transformation Books
211 Pauline Drive #513
York, PA 17402
www.TransformationBooks.com

ISBN: 978-0-9968271-5-7
Library of Congress Control No: 2016935657

Cover design by: Ranilo Cabo *with creative inspiration provided by*
 Donald Middleton
Layout and typesetting: Ranilo Cabo
Editor: Allison Saia
Proofreader: Michelle Cohen
Book Midwife: Carrie Jareed

Printed in the United States of America

CONVERSATIONS
with my
DAD

Accessing your full potential by making the right choices at the right time.

Dedication

Dedicated to everyone who protects us daily with honor and integrity. Especially to the men and women of the armed forces, who continuously sacrifice time away from their loved ones so that we can continue be safe.

Table of Contents

Dedication v
Preface xi
Acknowledgments xiii
The Origin xiv
The Purpose xv
Letter to the Creator xvii

Chapter I
Mind Your Business 1
   You Are a Business 1
   Protecting Your Brand 3
   Credit 5
   Credit Management 7
   Establishing Credit 7
   Know Your Limitation 9
   Avoid Hype When Entering Into Business Agreement 12
   Understand Your Value 13
   How Self-Worth Affects Confidence 14
   Common Ideas That Distort Our Perception 15
   Four Factors That Influence Self-Worth 15
   What Is Your Most Valuable Asset? 17
   What's Your State of Mind 17
   Covering Your Assets 18
   Food For Thought 21

Chapter II
Why A Good Education Is A Necessity 23
   You Have To Pay For Your Education 23
   You Can Pay Me Now - Or You Can Pay Me Later .. 24
   School Is Just Not For Me 26
   Everyone Doesn't Learn the Same Way and
      at the Same Rate 26

Chapter III
The Keys to A Better Existence **33**
    Relationships 35
    Heredity vs. Environment 37
    Are You Tough Enough? 42
    Building Good Relationships 45
    Know-How 46
    Bullying 48

Chapter IV
The Importance of Choosing the
Right Mate/Partner **55**
    The Secret to a Long-Term Relationship 56
    Friend of the Court 58
    The Eyeball Test 59
    The Tie That Binds You 61

Chapter V
The Importance of Maintaining Your
Family Structure **65**
    The African American Perspective 67
    Perspective 68
    Dad's Responsibility 69
    Dad The Protector 70
    Mom, The First Protector 72
    Mom The Teacher 72
    Mother's Strength 73
    Message from Dad to Daughter 74
    Who is in Your Family? 75

Chapter VI
The Importance of Good Negotiation Skills **77**
    Leverage 80
    Why Negotiate? 80
    Buying Power 82

Chapter VII
Choices (Race/Religion/Politics) 85
    Race 85
    Friends and Race 96
    Race in America 96
    Religion 98
    Politics 101
    Transforming Your Political Landscape 101
    Messaging 102
    Getting Your Desired Political Outcome 102
    Final Thoughts 107
    Congratulations! 107

About The Author 109

Preface

The trials of life and a slow week for news gave birth to this father's guide for his children. I am a strong believer in the idea that history is shaped by the deeds of extraordinary men and women. This theory was most memorably advanced by the British writer, Thomas Carlyle, and was well-suited to the American version of this University of Detroit graduate.

Conversations with my Dad is insistent on the premise that people should take an honest look at the world surrounding them and create memorable forms of knowledge to enrich the lives of the young people they come in contact with each and every day. Although the topic implies Dad, it is built around the African parable: "It takes a village to raise a child." Therefore, the book's signature series tribute was not the result of high level philosophy; rather, it was driven by something far more important: Donald's historical deadline.

Acknowledgments

It took a lot of patience and expertise to bring this book from what was a dream into reality. I'd like to thank my wife, first and foremost, for her patience and nurturing, which inspired me to get this book done. I want to also thank my children who, through our life experiences, provided me much of the content that is discussed in this book. A special thanks to my sisters who helped mold and nurture me into a responsible man. Thank you to all of my brothers biological as well as those who took me under their wing and protected me as I evolved. I also would like to thank the members of Christine Kloser's publishing team, especially Allison and Carrie, who are almost as patient as my wife.

Thank You

The Origin

This book is based on conversations that I had with my sons. At the time, I saw one of my sons making bad decisions that I knew would impact his life negatively in the future. So I decided to sit down with both of them and record some important topics that I felt would be necessary in moving them towards future successful outcomes.

The topics that we covered were:
- Mind your business
- Why a good education is a necessity
- The keys to a better existence/conflict resolution
- The importance of choosing the right mate/partner
- The importance in maintaining you family structure
- The importance of good negotiation skills
- Choices (Race Religion and Politics)

I chose these topics as a foundation of what I felt would be an ongoing and continuing dialogue for them as they moved forward into manhood. As we cover each of these topics individually, I will explain how each of them can be life-changing and transformational.

The Purpose

Conversations with My Dad was designed for individuals who feel that they are not getting their desired outcomes and who have determined that change is necessary.

- Keep in mind, in order for any method used to gain success, an individual or group must be willing to do the following things.
- Take an honest inventory of their current life circumstances and how they arrived at them.
- Visualize where they would like their transformation to take them.
- Map out a strategy for achieving your desired outcome.
- Commit yourself to your cause (DISCIPLINE).

"Success is to be measured not so much by the position that one has reached in life as by the obstacles which he has overcome."

Booker T. Washington

Letter to the Creator

God,

Today I am seeking understanding. As I go through this life that I have been given charge of, I understand that I am to give you all honor and praise. After that, I honestly don't understand how it works. It's as if someone has given me a great gift without proper or complete instructions. Many claim to have the answers, which are laid out in the many different texts that have been written over time. However, what I have come to find over the years, is that many of these writings have been altered or changed in order to serve the purposes of the individuals that are promoting them. I know that everything that I, and the many inhabitants of this world, need to live a righteous life has already been placed within us at birth. What I am trying to understand is, why do the good have to suffer with the bad? Why does it always seem as though the bad prosper while the righteous struggle? Why do so many good people have to die so young? God, I know you know my heart; but I have a confession to make. I stand before you as humbly as I know how and I want you to know that I am angry. Well, to be honest, I'm not only angry; I'm also confused. Why? It's because I see so many young people murdered or corrupted before they even get a chance to experience life. This shouldn't be and I know you have your reasons, but this has left me, and so many others like me, with burning questions.

This reality leads me to ask these questions:

1. Are we your personal experiment?
2. Were we put here just to see who will survive and who will be consumed by the evil nature of mankind?
3. Or are we in a hell that we will never escape?

Too often I hear about the abuses of man and how they cry out for your intervention; and many times it seems as though these calls or prayers go unanswered.

I want everyone who reads these words that I have written today to know that I have no doubt that God almighty is real and does exist. I just don't understand how the Creator works.

Many people will read this and will try to explain how you operate, but I have come to find out that they really don't fully understand any of it either.

Before I close, I want you to know what I do understand is this; each and every one of us is here for a reason and we all have contributions that we will leave in this world.

I chose to make a good contribution, so I am sitting here today finishing the work I started so long ago.

May the words that you inspire me to write, help many people along their journeys in this life and become a positive influence for many years to come.

Amen.

Thank you for your patience!

Chapter I

Mind Your Business

Businesses are usually defined by their mission statement. A mission statement is a brief description of a company's fundamental purpose. It answers the question, "Why do we exist?" The mission statement articulates the company's purpose both for those in the organization and for the public. What's your mission statement?

You Are a Business
You need to understand this first and foremost: you are a business and everything you do helps people to understand how you operate, what your purpose is and why they should include you in their life. In other words, you are your BRAND.

As we go through life, we enter into business transactions and agreements every day. People sometimes see us individually as a means to their end or to put it in other words, people do business asking the infamous question, "What can you do for me?"

Whether you want to believe it or not, that is the agreement many of us work under daily. Think about it. We start our process at a young age. We go to school, and as we work our way through this process in our life, we are trying to decide how we want to earn our living as an adult. Some people go to college to build their brand, in an effort to land a good-paying job in an established business, while some people choose the path of an entrepreneur.

Whatever choice you settle on during your development, you must realize that you are building your brand. As it relates to people seeing you as a means to their end, consider this: Once you have completed all of your schooling, you then set out in the effort of seeking gainful employment. When you sit down to interview for a job, your potential employer is evaluating you to see if the two of you are a good fit. At this stage of the interview process, the interviewer is evaluating your brand and trying to see if you are a good fit for their posted position.

However, this should not be a one-sided evaluation process; you should also be evaluating your potential employer as well, with the intent of making sure that you are involving yourself in a win-win situation.

Everything you do in life determines how your brand is developed and viewed by others.

Let's start from the beginning. As you grow and develop during your childhood years, you need to understand that the decisions you make will have an impact on your future. That's why it's important to always put your brand in the best position that you possibly can.

Whether you want to believe it or not, many of the things that you did as a child have a direct impact on your current life situation. This includes the good, the bad and the ugly. The good may have been a personal relationship that you developed early on which presented you with some great opportunities. The bad may have been some encounters that you had with the law that are prohibiting you from getting a job that you are applying for. The ugly may stem from some negative treatment that you gave another individual and you now have to deal with the repercussion from it.

Keep this in mind as you make your journey on your life's pathway. Everything you choose to do has repercussions that come along with it. The thing that you need to determine when making tough choices or any choice for that matter is: "Am I willing to live with the outcome from the choice?"

In today's world, it seems that almost everything we do gets monitored and because of this, it very important to consider just who is watching and why. You never know when you'll be in a video or photo on someone's social media page. For example, one of the things that we have grown to love (and some feel that they just can't live without) is our cell phone. Many people never stop to think just how much of their personal brand and business information they are giving away for free just by having this device on them. Cell phones are also used to track you, to monitor your buying habits and to identify your personal contacts. Little do many people know, this is done when you agree to add many of the apps that you download. (Read the fine print.) We use these devices to send and receive messages, pictures, and many other things. Some people have lost good careers because of the messages and pictures that they have sent with this device. Keep this in mind and think twice before you hit send. More importantly, if you have to think more than twice, you probably shouldn't send it. Don't forget to ask yourself: Am I willing to live with the repercussions? Am I doing everything I can to protect my brand?

By thinking things through, you're sure to become more aware of your actions. Our world has become so digitized that the things we used to view as routine and harmless are now more serious and strategic.

Protecting Your Brand

While having a chat with my sons one day, the topic of unpaid parking tickets came up. I explained to my sons why they needed to address all ticket matters immediately and in the appropriate fashion. I wanted to make it abundantly clear how their brand would be damaged if those matters went ignored. Unpaid tickets are one of the quickest and potentially costliest ways to unconsciously hurt your brand. They usually lead to a damaging chain of events: from additional fees, suspended driving privileges and potentially to a warrant being issued for your arrest. Many people learn this too late. However, you need to address this business matter immediately before it becomes life-altering to your brand. Unfortunately, my sons wanted to learn this the hard way.

One day, while standing around with a group of their friends, they were issued tickets for loitering. Neither of them addressed the matter immediately, which caused it to snowball into a larger issue. Sometime later, while in the process of a traffic stop, my son was informed by the officer that he had a warrant for unpaid tickets. My son told the officer he didn't have any traffic violations, at which time the officer informed him the warrant was not for a traffic stop, but for a loitering ticket. My son then had an "Ah-ha and oh boy moment." The one thing that he thought was no big deal at the time was putting him into a situation where he could be arrested. This is why you should always be aware of your business and your business standing.

You need to know that the recipe for a successful brand includes carefully defining what your business represents and delivering a positive customer experience every time. Whatever your business may be, your brand says, "This is who I am and this is what I can do for you." The stronger the brand, the greater the correlation is to the person that you seek to do business with.

Creating, promoting and protecting your brand is the role that you should be heavily involved in. Protecting your brand, which is your marketplace identity, starts with careful brand management. Your brand may have started as a name, but over time your brand identity may include a variety of things that you have been associated with along your journey. It shows up in the quality that you consistently deliver when interacting with others.

Your brand is the most valuable piece of your business structure and without proper care and attention, it could become damaged or disappear completely. Protecting your brand use and maintaining its consistency across interactions and locations is the single most important objective for you.

The best place to start protecting your brand is when you first develop your business strategy. Equally important to protecting a brand is that you, as an individual business entity, keep the promises made by your brand and maintain the positive reputation and image with the people that you interact with daily. Your brand should be at the top of your mind in every decision that you make about how you do business.

You'll never totally control how the people perceive your brand. You can, however, influence the people's perception of your brand by carefully guarding your reputation.

The stronger your brand is, the more likely you are to survive unplanned, and potentially catastrophic, situations. Here are some keys to protecting your brand:

- Your brand needs to be "top-of-mind" in every decision you make about your business affairs.
- Market your brand – those around you do and so should you.
- Work on your brand in an effort to strengthen it.
- Keep your brand message consistent.
- Set yourself apart and above the competition by emphasizing what is distinctive about the brand and what is better.
- Never get too comfortable. A top brand can quickly lose its pull.

Credit

Credit is short for the word creditability. When you have good creditability, business matters seem to go a lot smoother.

Credit can be used as a major part of building your successful brand. It is a business tool that needs to be monitored and protected. When you are in good credit standing, many of your business tasks and transactions run much smoother. Don't forget what was said earlier, "Some people see you as a business opportunity." These same people would much rather do business with people that they deem trust and creditworthy.

The opposite is true when your creditability is bad. It's not normal for people to try to do bad things with their credit. Sometimes this occurs after the loss of a job or income or after making a bad choice. Another thing that hurts your credit more than you think is not paying back student loans.

Most people don't understand what the impact is for ignoring this debt. Some student loans are backed by the government which means, in the end, they are going to get their money back. This sometimes comes in the form of the IRS holding the tax refund that you were so looking forward to getting, or placing a derogatory mark on your credit report, which then makes it more difficult for you to get future credit or loans at a favorable rate. Don't forget credit, like all of your other business dealings, should have a component of a win-win built within it. Here is what I mean: you, as a consumer of credit, are entering into an agreement with the lender. In return for letting you use their money, the lender then receives interest which is paid over the time period of the loan. If the terms of the agreement are not favorable to you, then you may need to seek other options.

Keeping your credit as clean as possible will save you money in the long run. Here is an example: two people go into a car dealership to buy the same car and get the car loan. During this particular month, the dealer is offering zero down and a zero percent interest rate. Here is the key phase of the offer statement: "For qualified buyers." What that means is, if your credit score is a certain number, you can get that vehicle for the offered deal. However, if your credit score falls outside of that range, you need to be prepared to pay more money for the same vehicle, if you are going to use their credit offerings.

Buying more than you can afford to pay back is another credit killer. As I drive around town, I see many people driving new vehicles and when I ask most people are they happy with their purchase? The reply that I get is, "I love my car, but I hate my payment." In other words, many people are riding around with buyer's remorse.

You can avoid being one of those individuals that has buyer's remorse by minding your business, preparing yourself before entering into long-term agreements and keeping in mind that there will always be another deal at a later time.

Credit Management
Your credit history is a list of all the pieces of your financial life. It includes every credit card account you've opened and any other loans you've taken out. It also includes your debt repayment history.

Many factors can affect your credit score, including whether you've paid on time or not, been foreclosed upon or filed for bankruptcy. If a court has ordered you to repay a loan or your debt has been deemed uncollectible-these, too, affect your score. All of this information stays on your credit history for a certain amount of time.

Lenders look at your credit history to assess your ability to pay back their money. If you are having money problems, you represent greater risk to a lender. The basic principle with credit is this: use credit wisely and spend within your means.

Establishing Credit
If you don't have credit (or much credit), the key is to start small. One credit card or small loan can get the ball rolling. But make sure your lender reports your on-time payments to one of the three credit bureaus- ExperianSM (experian.com), Equifax (equifax.com) or TransUnion® (transunion.com)-and preferably to all three. If your on-time payments don't get reported, you're accumulating debt, but not building credit.

Only credit accounts that report your borrowing and repayment activity will count toward your credit history. Here are some tips to help you establish a good credit history:

- When establishing credit, pay off your charges in full at the end of the month. Always pay off the balance in full when the statement arrives. This shows the card company that you're fiscally responsible. You're using credit as it was intended, as a short-term loan.

- Pay on time. One of the most important steps in building and maintaining a solid credit history is to pay all of your bills on time each month. By paying on time, you're showing the lender or creditor that you've got enough cash flow to cover your expenses. If you pay late and the creditor reports your late payment to the credit bureaus, it may damage your credit history and lower your credit score.
- Keep your total charges well within your credit limit. If you want to boost your credit history and credit score, you'll want to keep your total monthly charges well within your credit limit. Why? In calculating your credit score, you'll take a hit if your balance is above that limit, because it signals to creditors that you may be having financial difficulties and thus are a riskier borrower.
- Read your credit report regularly. One way to building a positive credit history is to make sure you know what information is being reported. Errors and negative information can damage your credit history and your credit score, so you'll want to regularly check your credit report to see what's there.
- Understand what debit cards can do for you. While they look like credit cards, debit cards actually function more like a checkbook. They provide direct access to the cash in your bank account. So you can pay for items and services with a debit card instead of writing a check. What debit cards *don't* do is help you build your credit history. That's because you're not using credit to buy these items—you're using something that's treated like cash. Because you're using a cash substitute instead of credit, your debit card activity isn't reported to the credit bureaus and won't help you establish good credit.

- Consider getting a secured credit card. A secured credit card is tied to an account. You deposit a certain amount of money into the account and then you can charge up to that amount. If you default on your payment, the bank can tap into the account to get repaid. After six to 12 months of on-time payments, you may feel you're ready to graduate to a regular credit card or a store card. However, resist the urge to open too many store card accounts just to take advantage of discounts. Every time you open one, it results in a credit report inquiry, which may affect your score.
- Ask for a credit line increase. After you've had your first credit card for a while (six months to a year), call the issuer and ask to increase your credit limit. The idea is to raise the credit limit on the card, not your debt load. If you're carrying a balance, raising your limit will help keep your debt-to-credit-limit ratio low. That's an important factor when calculating a credit score.
- Focus on what you want. Your credit history becomes critical when it's time to make those big purchases, like a home or a car. At that point, a one percent difference in the interest on a loan will either cost you or save you thousands of dollars over the life of the loan.
- By keeping your eye on the goal-establishing and maintaining a good credit history, you'll be able to borrow that money when you want it, at the most favorable terms and conditions being offered.

Know Your Limitation

A main component of minding your business or building your brand, is knowing your limitations. This is true in everything that you do in life. Let's say you're at the gym and you are lifting weights. While doing so, you add more weight than you are capable of lifting and injure yourself. (Not good) Adding more weight than you can handle happens not only at the gym, but also in life if you don't know your limitations.

We see something we want and we say that we will pay for it later. Well, sometimes later doesn't come in time and we end up putting a strain on our brand. This happens most often during the Christmas holiday. Many consumers get caught up in the branding, hype and pressures of the holiday season.

For example, you may see an electronic device that you have been eyeing for some time get marked down to a price that you like. Let's say at the time of the markdown you don't have the cash money to make the purchase. You may then think to yourself, "I will just put it on my credit card." However, if your credit card is close to being maxed out or if you are unable to pay off the purchase within the allotted grace period, then you really haven't saved anything at all. Since the interest that you will be paying will be wiping out any perceived gains from the markdown.

Another example of not understanding your limitations is buying more house than you need. You should avoid purchasing a large home to house a small amount of people. It is wise to not purchase a large vehicle that doesn't meet the needs of your driving conditions or circumstances. For example, buying a sports car for winter driving conditions or an SUV to zoom up and down the highway.

You should keep these words in mind when getting ready to spend your hard earned money: "People often spend money that they don't have, to buy things that they don't need, to impress people that they don't know."

Merchants, as I said earlier, see you as a means to their end, which in this case is profitability and getting into the black for the year. That's why the day after Thanksgiving is called Black Friday. You should try not to spend more than you can afford to pay back within the 30 day grace period of your credit card.

The soundest business advice that you should follow is the pay-as-you-go system. This is a good principle to follow when you are trying to stay practical and stay out of debt. Pay-as-you-go may seem a little more difficult when you are starting out with very little cash resources or support. But in the long run, it proves to be the most liberating decision that you will make.

I was at my dentist around Christmas time one year and my hygienist asked me, "What are you going to do for Christmas?" I told her that I already did it. She then asked, "What did you do?" I told her that I have paid off all of my debt and that I felt so free because of it.

She said, "I know what you mean, I had all of my debt paid off too and then like a dummy I went out and ran my credit cards up again."

I said, "Credit cards? You mean with an 's?' What do you need with more than one credit card?"

She said, "You know how you get one and then they send you more offers to get newer and better ones with lower interest rates and perks?"

I said, "Oh, you fell for that trick huh?" I went on to say, "They aren't usually giving you anything except for more burden to add to your financial woes."

If you don't maintain this additional credit properly you will find yourself overburdened with credit card debt. Lots of people have credit and do everything that is needed to keep their rating at a high level and that's how credit should be managed. I use the word "managed" because remember, we are talking about your business and you are the front line manager of it.

I understand that paying your credit card balance off within thirty days is easier said than done for many people; however you need to realize that there are times, that you are faced with extenuating circumstances. These times are usually related to making major purchases such as the purchase of a new home or car. Keep this in mind, a little proper planning and the adherence to your plan goes a long way in your avoiding long-term debt and high interest payments.

I don't know, if some people don't take the time to think, or if they really don't care about the implications of buying "so-called sales items" on credit. I say this because if you buy a sales item for 20 percent off, and you don't pay that sales item off before you're hit with the interest rate of your credit card, you actually lose on any savings that you may have been trying to get on that purchase.

Avoid hype when entering into business agreement

Hype is often used to sell you on a product or service, which often implies if you don't take the deal now, I can't guarantee that it will be available for you later. If you take the time to ask people that you know, "Have you ever bought something based on hype, and what was the outcome?" If they're honest with you, they will probably tell you that they were a little disappointed.

Here is an example of what I feel is a big sells hype pitch: **TIMESHARES.** When you attend a timeshare presentation, you are presented with many great tourist destinations and the relaxing and warm atmosphere that the destinations offer. You are told that you can become part owner of the shared property and its offerings. There is a lot of cheering, and a lot of celebrating revolving around trips that you haven't taken yet. Depending on your finances, you may never be able to take any of these trips. Most of all, there is a lot of hype related to these potential destinations. This is where and when many of the purchasers of the offering lose their focus. This loss of focus has led people into long-term agreements that they now find difficulty getting out of. Here is a place that MINDING YOUR BUSINESS would have gone a long way in protecting your brand and credit.

In my use of the timeshare example, I'm not saying that timeshares are a bad investment. I'm only saying that they are not for everyone that signs up for them. You need to understand that the salesperson is trying to make a sale and during that time, you should be protecting your business.

The most important thing that you have at your disposal and never hesitate to use it, is your ability to walk away.

Understand Your Value

This is where most people lose out on receiving their true worth. I bet we all know someone with a remarkable gift or talent, however they don't seem to know how to get the benefit from that talent. In order for you to benefit from your gifts or talent, you must first get an understanding of your value. In doing that, it will put you closer to where you need to be, in pursuit of receiving your benefits.

One day, while watching music videos with my children, I noticed that in almost every video, the artist would talk about what kind of clothing they were wearing or what type of vehicle they drove and even the type of alcohol that they consumed. I said to my children, "I bet they don't have an endorsement deal with any of those companies that they are speaking of; yet by doing so they are giving away free advertising." Companies understand the power of the spoken word and who delivers that word goes a long way in brand exposure and promotion. In other words, don't give your marketing machine away for nothing. Get your value!

How do you get your value? By understanding what's at stake, what kind of leverage that you have over the obstacles that you will be confronted with and how best to use your understanding and leverage.

While watching some of the same videos, one of my children asked me why are the words blurred on the clothing of the artist? I explained that this is usually done by the network because they don't have an endorsement deal with whatever item or product is being blocked out. There is no such thing as free advertising or brand promotion without some sort of compensation.

You should be doing the same thing when it comes to giving away your marketing machine or aligning your brand; make sure that you are receiving some sort of benefit for the marketing and promotions that you are involved in. Too often we do this without even giving it a second thought.

I recall taking my car to the dealer one day for service. After the service on my vehicle was completed, I noticed that I had the dealer's name framed around my license plate. I went to the service manager and asked, "Why is your dealership's name framed around my license plate?"

He replied, "We do that for our customers to let people know that you are a part of our dealerships sales and service group of customers."

I said, "Okay, that's great, but how much are you taking off of my bill today for me doing advertising for you?"

The service manager replied, "NOTHING," at which time I told him to have someone remove that from my car immediately.

You should know that there is nothing wrong with knowingly doing something to benefit others, but also keep in mind that there is also something to be said for reciprocity or mutual benefit.

How Self-worth Affects Confidence
Your confidence in your own abilities will ultimately be the deciding factor when it comes to taking action and producing results. A lack of self-confidence acts as a restraint, holding you back from pursuing the life that you desire. A distorted view of self-worth leads us to believe that we don't deserve a better life and undermines our efforts to create change.

Self-confidence, self-worth and self-esteem are all closely related and are based on a personal belief system. Beliefs are rarely about reality. They are an emotional conclusion based on our personal perception. This means that logic alone is not usually enough to alter limiting beliefs. But asking logical questions about the perceptions that lead to those beliefs can make them more susceptible to reason.

Common Ideas That Distort Our Perception
It's important to realize that there are those who work really hard to influence your views and personal values. Advertisers try to embed their product to our emotions in an effort to make

us feel incomplete, or below par, if you don't buy what they are selling.

Many employers want you to think that their approval is a key factor in your self-worth and that our job is the most important thing in your life. There is also a social perception that exerts a strong influence to live up to certain expectations. And these are just a few of the forces working to mold your viewpoints about yourself.

To counter some commonly accepted, but misguided notions about self-worth, let's take a closer look at the two sides of four different ideas that often lead to confusion.

Four Factors That Influence Self-Worth

1. **Someone else's opinion or your perception.** What this boils down to is whether you place greater importance on external or internal validation. I think that we all appreciate it when others approve of us, even if we have a strong sense of self-worth. It's human nature to want the approval of others, but it should not be the standard by which you gauge your own worth.

    You need to develop an empowering belief about your own self-worth as a person, and it should form the basis for your personal validation. Validation should be used to reinforce your beliefs, not as a basis for them.

    Never allow someone else's opinion of you to shape your view of yourself. You can build your sense of self-worth by giving sincere approval to yourself every single day.

2. **What you've acquired or what you have given.** How much stuff we own has absolutely nothing to do with our personal self-worth. Your contributions are much more important than your acquisitions. Giving from

the heart is a reflection of your inner self. It speaks of who you are, not how much you can afford.

Making personal value judgments based on material assets is for shallow thinkers only. Leave that thinking for the creditors. You don't want to think that way, and you don't need to be influenced by those who do.

3. **Accomplishments or efforts.** Accomplishment is a wonderful thing. Most people feel great when they work at something and get the results that they wanted. But here's the thing: sometimes they succeed at producing their intended result; and sometimes they fail. That's just a fact of life for everyone.

The problem is, the reward for success is usually tangible while the value of failure can be much harder to appreciate. Life is about learning what works and what doesn't. In the learning process, success and failure have equal value as long as we learn from them. Never link your self-worth to the results you produce. You are a person, not an accomplishment.

4. **Flash or substance**. This one seems obvious enough, and yet our culture often places greater value on flash. Never mistake looks, abilities, outrageous behavior or material wealth as a measure of self-worth. Substance is the name of the game. No matter how nicely wrapped a package is, the important thing is what's inside.

The same is true of people; it's what's inside that counts. When we are true to our personal ethics, we have integrity. When we care about the welfare of others, we have compassion. When we give without expecting anything in return, we are generous.

Cultivate these qualities and you will be a person of substance. What a wonderful basis for a strong sense of self-worth and feelings of personal value

What Is Your Most Valuable Asset?

You have something of great worth: and it is so rare that it's not shared by anyone else on the planet. Do you know what that is? You are a one of a kind, totally unique individual. You are you, and that alone gives you personal value and self-worth.

Take some time to appreciate who you really are, aside from all the trappings and outside opinions. Make a list of things you like about yourself and then read it out loud so it can resonate in your consciousness. Think about all the ways you have contributed to the lives of those around you. Now, give yourself some well-deserved approval. You need to celebrate you!

What's Your State of Mind

Before entering into any business agreement, partnership, or purchase, you should always make sure that you are in the right state of mind. Let me explain why. When you make decisions while in the wrong state of mind, the choices that you made during that period usually aren't the best ones that you could have made for long-term success.

Here are a couple of examples. It is said that you should never go grocery shopping on an empty stomach. Why, because everything in the store looks good and you want it and you want it now. This is because you are in the wrong state of mind for grocery shopping. When you're hungry, your stomach is sending a message to your brain that I want food and I want food now. While this is taking place, you may start to engage in impulse shopping. Impulse shopping usually leads to you buying things that you had not intended to get at the time.

Another example is when a person goes out to make a major purchase like a car or a home; you need to really make sure that your state of mind is right doing these processes, or you will probably end up leaving the deal paying much more than you had planned. Professional sales people are aware of this and many of them take advantage of your desires and impulses during this critical time.

This happens to almost everyone when they make any substantial purchase, it's called upselling and we all have probably fallen victim to it at one time or another. Here is what usually happens: we buy a good or service and at the time of payment or some time right before payment we are asked, "Would you like to by the protection plan or extended warranty?" This is where the profitability starts for the merchant. Many purchases don't require the need for extra added protection because many time it's covered by the manufacturer.

That's not to say, don't buy a warranty and nor am I implying that we, as consumers, should take the anti-salesperson approach. What I am simply trying to do is to let you know that it's in your best interest to be well-informed, prepared and in the right state of mind before you spend your hard-earned money. Once again, remember, the salesperson is trying to make a living by selling their product or services and you are in the business of maximizing and protecting your brand.

Covering Your Assets

Just like any other business, your business assets are going to need to be protected. Say for instance, you owned a store or some kind of retail shop that deals with the public. As a shop owner you know that certain things need to be put in place for the security and overall health of your business. This is no different for you as a business, you need to cover your personal health to make sure that you are running at your peak. This needs to be done by making sure that you have a family physician that understands the history of you and your family's personal health.

Whether you want to believe it or not, your health is your wealth. Ask any cash-rich person that may be dying from an incurable disease or an inoperable condition. Ask them this: "If you could trade in all of your money for perfect health, would you do it?" I bet you, overwhelmingly, the answer would be yes. Because you can always find ways to accumulate more money, but you can't always regain or find good health.

In the effort of covering your business you must get checkups along the way. I know for men this is often something that they avoid. However, if they want to see their business create and maintain long-term success under their leadership, then they need to do maintenance on themselves just like they do maintenance on their car or any other asset that they are trying to preserve.

Know and understand your family history. When you have a better understanding of some of the things that have affected your family members over the course of their lives, this will give you a heads up for things to look for as you begin to age as well. If your family has a history of heart conditions, then it's probably in your best interest to eat healthy, exercise and get regular checkups to help you maintain good heart health. This goes for any other condition that may be passed down through your gene pool.

Another component that should be included in the covering of your business is finding or knowing a good and honest attorney. Believe me when I tell you this: the best time to find an attorney is when you don't need one. I say this because when many individuals get into a legal situation, they get an attorney based on the recommendation of a friend or family member and not through research and planning.

Let me share a story about how this once happened to me. I told you of my dear son who inspired this book. Well, one day he found himself in a legal situation that required an attorney. I called a friend of mine who recommended an attorney that he used to help him with a legal matter. The attorney told me, based on my son's situation and the fact that he had never been in trouble before, that he could get everything taken care of for three thousand dollars. I agreed to this amount and we went to court. Once in court my son, along with his bad business partner, entered the court room. My son had a paid attorney and his business partner had a court-appointed attorney. The charges are read. The two attorneys present their positions: and both my son and his business partner get community service and probation based on their legal history. At this point I start thinking to myself, "Gee, my son's business partner got the same result as him and he didn't have to pay three thousand dollars." I truly paid for not knowing!

After discussing this with other legal minds, I discovered that this is a common sentence for first-time offenders. I also learned that what the attorney charged me was not the reasonable and customary charge for the services rendered. However, keep in mind as I said earlier: I agreed to the amount. So that's what I get for not minding my business. Even though it's no consolation to me, the attorney that I discussed in my example was later convicted for tax fraud and illegal business practices. I learned a much more valuable lesson. That being, you should always do your due diligence by having the right people in the right place for circumstances that may come up in business and in life.

I don't want you to think by giving the above example that I am implying that attorneys are bad people, although many people would beg to differ. I'm trying to get you to understand how things can go wrong, if you aren't protecting your brand.

Most large corporations and businesses have attorneys that they retain for any legal matter that may arise. Even though you are not a big business, you should always have someone in mind if you are looking for legal help to cover your brand.

Have you ever been in a situation or have you seen someone on the news that has been involved in an unfortunate situation? The last thing that a person wants to hear after or during a disaster is, "You're not covered for that." Make sure you are covered for whatever the situation arises in your life.

Food For Thought

I'm going to throw this tidbit in for you to consider if you become a parent and are raising a child of your own.

"Your goals and dreams are not your children's goals and dreams."

You may say, what do you mean by that? Here is what I'm saying. When children are born, many parents try to set up a life for their child, based on the future that they would like them to have. While that is not a bad thing, many parents never take the time to ask their children, what it is they THINK they want for their future. As a parent, I understand that most grownups don't even know what they want out of life and their future. However, what I'm trying to get you to think about from a parental perspective is this, "Am I investing my time and effort in the right place?"

On a personal note, here is what happened to my wife and me. We are both sport lovers and players. In an effort to expose our children to the sports that we love, we took our children to sporting events that we participated in. Hoping that someday, they too would grasp a genuine love for it. However we found out that, yes, they too liked sports, but not as much as we did. Here is another example. We both have always had a drive toward entrepreneurialism and exposed our children to business and business models. We later learned that they were not interested in being business owners.

I'm saying all of this in hopes of saving you from making an investment in time and money that may not give you the return that you are seeking. In short, enjoy your time as you grow with your children and make the life adjustments that come along the way, because your future will not necessarily be their future.

Keep this in mind as you go through life: everything that you do has an impact on you brand. The decisions that you consciously and unconsciously make will determine whether the path that you walk in life is a smooth one or a rough one.

Chapter II

Why A Good Education Is A Necessity

To educate or not to educate, that is the question. Here is the answer: EDUCATE. Education helps you in getting the know how, that will lead you to greater success. There are many forms of education and different ways to receive it. It doesn't matter how you get it, just get it. Don't wait until late in the game to get your education. You should have been educating yourself all of the time. Do it every day, in whatever it is that you do.

You Have To Pay For Your Education

I remember a story that one of my Army buddies told me one day while we were deployed in the field. He asked me if I knew how to shoot dice? I explained to him that I didn't. He was puzzled and asked me, "How could you grow up in Detroit and not know how to shoot dice?" I went on to explain to him that my father did not allow any kind of gambling or card games for stakes to be played in or around the house. My friend asked me if I wanted to learn how to play? I said I wasn't interested, because from what I could remember about most street dice games is that they always ended up in a dispute over the money and some of them didn't end well. Now you may be asking yourself what does this have to do with education.

As we began to discuss playing dice amongst each other, my buddy told the story of how he learned how to play dice. He said one day as a young kid, he saw the older guys playing and asked if he could play. My buddy said one of the guys told him if he wanted to play that he would have to pay for his education. He asked the guy how much it would cost. The guy then asked him how much money he had. He said fifty dollars. The guy said that was a good start, and told him to have a seat. He told my buddy it cost five dollars to buy in.

They began to play the game and my buddy started losing his money. While in the process of losing his money, he said the other guy would shake the dice, and say, "Don't forget you got to pay for your education." By not being educated in the art or rules of the game, my buddy eventually lost all of his money. Thank goodness that it was only fifty dollars and not his life.

Know-how and education. Are you beginning to see how they go together? Know-how becomes a more powerful tool when you properly educate yourself. Education must always be paid for in some fashion or form: be it time, money or both. When you are young, you usually pay for your education with your time and some other person's money. This is true in most cases of children in grades K through 12, unless you are in a private school where someone is paying out cash for your education. It all still boils down to you paying for your education. Here is a little advice: It's much better to learn on someone else's dime while contributing only your time.

You Can Pay Me Now - Or You Can Pay Me Later

I recall having a conversation with my son during his younger years. I was explaining to him why he should go to school and that these will probably be some of the best times of his life. I told him to just live in the moment and take in all of the good things that time period has to offer. I wanted him to understand that he should enjoy the journey and quit concentrating on the destination.

My son at the time was not trying to hear that. All he wanted to remind me of was that he was going to the NBA. I said that's interesting, since in order to get in the NBA you had to go to school, even if just for a short period of time. My son being the little knuckle-headed rebel that he is (got that honestly from his father) said, "I'm going to the pros as soon as I finish high school."

I said, "You poor little misguided soul. Let's do the math, which happens to be something that you need to get better at. There are thirty NBA teams. They have an active roster of twelve guys, with maybe three more guys in an inactive reserve role. So let's just say roughly 450 players, out of those 450 spots, you have millions of guys with your same goal and dream in mind. So what differentiates you from them?"

My son said, "I'm better."

I replied, "That's interesting, because those other guys are saying the same thing, except for the fact that they are going to school and sharpening their skills." My son tells me that he is going to be better than Michael Jordan. I had to make my son aware of one thing, that Jordan was not necessarily the best basketball player ever, but he may well have been the best player that the system ever produced. My son asked me what I meant by that. I explained to him that I had played with guys who had equal or even better skills than Jordan, however they did not finish school or made bad life choices, which lead to them never fulfilling their potential. Although they were some of the best basketball players never to be discovered, their lack of education and life choices didn't afford them the opportunity or exposure to play professionally.

School Is Just Not For Me

I don't know how many times that I have heard this comment, but I do know one thing: it has been the mindset that has limited so many people from bringing their gifts to the masses. Going back to one of my basketball experiences, I recall playing at a gym one day, and as we were warming up, one of the guys that was about six feet tall just took off, leapt through the air and dunked the ball effortlessly. I was in awe, because not only could he "jump out of the gym," he also could score and play defense very well. After we played, I asked him, "Why aren't you playing college ball somewhere?"

His reply was, "School is just not for me."

I said, "But man, you're better than most of the people that I watch on TV."

He said, "Yeah, but I don't like school."

Far too many times, young people lose interest in the school system due to outside influences, learning disabilities and labeling. This is unfortunate, because with just a little more help or a little more guidance, their personal skill sets could be unlocked along with their ability to grasp concepts.

Everyone Doesn't Learn the Same Way and at the Same Rate

I am sure you have heard people criticize athletes for not being smart, as it relates to some of the circumstances that they find themselves in. Well, there are two sides to that coin. Sometimes an athlete's gift is just that, athletics. We should not expect a person gifted with enormous athletic ability to be as smart or possess the common sense of everyday people, no more than we should expect people who excel as an academic to possess the physical skills that will make them into a professional athlete.

Our learning model is flawed in that it expects a group of students to learn and advance at the same rate over a period of time. What it fails to do is move students along that are progressing at a rapid rate. The current system also doesn't hold students back as much as needed, so that they can get the extra time needed to learn. The education system does do this sometimes, but it just doesn't do it enough.

It also needs to be taken into account that everyone doesn't learn the same way. Some people are hands-on and need to interact physically within their learning environment, whereas others need to take a more cerebral approach. There is no particular way that is right or wrong. The bottom line is just learn as much as you can, no matter how you receive and retain knowledge. Make it a routine to learn something new every day.

As time passed, my son saw his NBA dreams fading away. I don't know if this played a part in his decision, but when he got to the twelfth grade, he dropped out of school. This is the main reason I stated before, why we sat down and did the *Conversations with My Dad* CD. I wanted him to have a record of all of the things that I tried to educate him on, but at the time he wasn't ready to receive. This ties into my topic of everyone doesn't learn the same way and at the same rate.

Fast forward to present day, I was having another coaching session with my son and he said to me, "Man, Pops, I should have completed college by now, I'm almost thirty years old and I'm just now getting a degree in higher learning." I replied that he should be glad that he is getting a chance to finish and build on what he started. After all, there are a lot of people who never got a chance to make right the wrongs that they have caused themselves.

I'm so happy to know that he now understands the value of a good education. Soon, he'll be able to say to his own children, complete your education early and throughout your lifetime and continue to educate yourself.

Here are some reasons why education is extremely important:

- **Overcoming Ignorance**
  Ignorance is baseless, useless and may affect your life negatively. Illiterate and uneducated people often tend to hold certain uninformed beliefs. Education and awareness are the best ways to combat ignorance and replace such beliefs with reason and logic.

- **Keeping up with the world**
  We live in an ever-changing world. New technologies keep coming up and if you don't want to be left behind, you must keep up with the fast-moving world. Without education, it will be really difficult for you to adapt to all these changes. An educated person is much more aware of the latest technologies and all the changes that are taking place in the world. For example, an uneducated person may not know about the benefits of the internet, whereas an educated person uses this gift of technology regularly for work as well as for entertainment.

- **Education and healthcare**
  Illiteracy often breeds ignorance and this ignorance may prove to be dangerous when it comes to healthcare. Educated people know better about preventive methods which protect them from a number of diseases. An illiterate and ignorant person is more likely to ignore the symptoms and avoids seeking medical aid unless the problem becomes very serious. Hence, education enables you to take better care of yourself as well as your family.

- **Respect**
  Everybody likes a wise and knowledgeable person! Educated people are considered highly reputable in society. The more educated you are, the more respect you will get from those around you.

- **Helps you understand the world we live in**
  Education helps you understand the what, when and where about the world you live in. You get to know more about your surroundings, as well as the whole world through subjects like history, geography, science, etc.

- **Makes the world a safer and more peaceful place**
  Education really affects our understanding of the difference between right and wrong. An educated person is well aware of the consequences of wrong/illegal actions and he or she is less likely to get influenced and do something which is not legally/morally right. Also, a number of uneducated people who live a poverty-stricken life owning to lack of opportunities often turn to illegal ways such as theft and robbery to solve their problems. If you are educated, you are well aware of your rights, the law and your responsibilities towards the society. Hence, education is an important factor which contributes in social harmony and peace.

- **Makes you confident**
  Your educational degree is considered as a proof of your knowledge by many. If you are educated, you have more chances of being heard and taken seriously. Generally, an uneducated person will find it harder to express his views and opinions owning to lack of

confidence. Even if he or she does so, people may not take you seriously. Education gives you the confidence to express your views and opinions.

- **Society**
  We all live in a society which has its own set of spoken/unspoken rules; and one of them is education. The society expects you to go to school, followed by college, get a job and settle down. In fact, education helps you become a useful member of the society. An educated member certainly has a greater chance to contribute to his community. Education helps you become an active member of the society and participate in the ongoing changes and developments.

- **For economic growth of the nation**
  Countries with very high literacy rates are extremely prosperous; and the citizens have a high per capita income. On the other hand, in underdeveloped and developing nations where literacy rate is not as high, a number of people are still living below the poverty line. Education is vital for the economic prosperity of a nation!

- **Saves you from being fooled/cheated**
  Education saves you from being exploited and fooled. We live in a country where we enjoy a number of rights and freedom. It is easier to take advantage of innocent and illiterate people. They may be trapped into signing false documents or be deprived of some right which they have because, unlike an educated person, they are not well aware of their rights and freedoms.

- **Turns your dreams into reality**
  What is your dream, your aim in life? Do you want to become rich? Do you want to be popular? Do you want to be an extremely successful person who is respected by people? Well, the key to all this is education. Of course there are exceptions, like sportsmen who don't really owe their success to their education. However, in most cases, your degree is what helps you realize all your dreams.

- **Helps you to become more independent**
  Education is very important if you want to be a self-dependent person. It helps you become financially independent, but that is not all. Education also makes you wiser so that you can make your own decisions.

- **Equality**
  If we want to see the world as a just and fair place where everyone is given equal opportunities, education is what we require. Education is a must if we want to do away with the existing differences between different social classes and genders. It opens a whole world of opportunities for the poor so that they may have an equal shot at well-paying jobs. Education also plays a major role in the empowerment of women.

- **Money**
  An educated person has more chances of landing up a good high paying job. Everybody wants a good life! Money may be called as the "root of all evil," but most people will agree that money is important for survival in today's world. The more educated you are, the better career options you have!

- **Education will go a long way in achieving a happy and stable life**
  If you want to lead a happy life and enjoy the good things the world has to offer, you certainly need to get educated. A great job, a good social reputation are few of the many benefits of being an educated person. Education is a good starting point for a promising and secure future and a stable life.

"THINK ABOUT IT. NOW GO AND GET IT!"

Chapter III

The Keys to A Better Existence

As we go on our journey through life, it is a natural phenomenon that we move just like electricity and take the path of least resistance. Throughout my life journey, I discovered two things that makes a person's existence better. Those two things are good **relationships** and **know-how**.

The reason this proves to be true more times than not, is because positive relationships with others usually lead to positive outcomes. The same thing can be said for negative relationships.

Think about it, many of the outcomes that people experience are based on the individual or group of individuals that they encounter daily. For instance, two people go into a job interview, both assuming that they have an equal chance at landing a particular job. However during the interview process, the interviewer finds out that one of the interviewees is his fraternity brother. That relationship alone (be it right or wrong) usually gives one person an advantage over the other, simply based on the positive relationship that the interviewer had either with the interviewee or someone the two knew in common. This can also go the other way as well. Let's change the circumstance and say the interviewer and the interviewee use to work together in the past. However, the interviewer left the old place of employment because of a negative relationship with the interviewee. The likelihood of the interviewee landing the job goes down drastically because of a past negative relationship. Those are a couple of ways that relationships can work for or against you.

Good relationships can present you with opportunities that open various pathways to future growth and success.

Here's another short story for you. The son of a friend was in need of a job, so I used the good relationship that I had with the interviewer to get him an interview and a possible inside track to the job. Keep this in mind, the inside track doesn't guarantee you the victory that you are seeking; it just gives you a better chance of winning. Also remember you still have to do your part. This is something that my friend's son did not do; he did not do his part. Before I set him up with the interview, I told him, "Look, you had better have your stuff together because they check everything when you are in the hiring process. They do a criminal background check, a drug screening and they check your driving record. Have all of those things been properly addressed?"

The young man told me, "Yes, sir, I don't have anything that will impact me negatively."

I said, "Alright, because you know that however you turn out good or bad that they are going to link us together so you had better shine when the opportunity presents itself."

The short of the story is that my friend's son did not get the job, because when they did his background check, he had a warrant for a ticket that he had gotten two years prior. You can imagine how I felt when I got that news. Everything eventually got straightened out, but that opportunity was missed because he didn't mind his business thoroughly.

(MIND YOUR BUSINESS) I can't stress enough how regular business checkups will go a long way in saving yourself from grief and embarrassment.

Relationships

I want to provide you with some examples of how relationships shape our lives. As I sit here writing this book today, American law enforcement and the African American community are at odds because of a long and documented history of bad relationships. This has led to unwanted attention for the law enforcement community and a chance for the African American community to get its message across and for its frustrations to be heard.

Let's start with a fictional scenario from one of my favorite childhood shows, *Andy Griffith*. In this show, there was a town drunk named Otis. Otis would, without fail, always land in jail for his excessive drinking. Since the officers of this town did not feel threatened by Otis and his actions, they would allow him to sleep off his drunkenness in a jail cell and let himself out of the jail when he sobered up. This could be done for what I see are several reasons.

1. Otis and the local authorities had a relationship that was developed over time and through that relationship the police officials felt that they could handle Otis in a particular way and still keep him and the town safe.
2. Also, by this being a small community, it was more than likely that there was some sort of good relationship in place, before Otis became what he had evolved into and the same with the officers. Good relationship being the key word here.

I used that example because I believe that one of the main issues that play a role in the relationship between law enforcement and the African American community is the relationship and the way it evolved.

There are numerous communities where the relationship law enforcement and the African American community work well. However, the anger that currently exists is due to law enforcement's excessive force, unfair treatment and the lack of accountability for those acts.

Trust and cooperation are parts of a relationship that are built over time through the positive and negative experiences that two parties encounter together and how they are resolved.

During an investigation, the police come to the citizens of the community asking for help in solving a crime. This interaction is usually met with resistance from the community, because they either don't want to get involved or they feel that law enforcement won't adequately protect them after they have cooperated. This can be very frustrating to law enforcement who sometimes say, "How can we help you if you are not willing to cooperate with us." In other instances, communities are asked, "How do you expect things to get better if you are not willing to speak up against the bad guys that cause trouble in your community?" That's a double-edged sword that most people don't want to pick up out of fear of retaliation.

Let's flip the circumstances around and see it from another point of view. Let's say that there is an officer on the police force and this officer has engaged in some questionable or unprofessional behavior. Once this behavior is exposed and brought before the public, all that most citizens are asking for is an honest and open due process. When this is not done, trust and credibility are damaged and even worse, may be lost forever. You can't expect the party that you are dealing with to be transparent, if you are perceived to be a protector of wrong doing and less cooperative when someone that you hold in high regard is involved in questionable actions. This type of behavior will lead to further mistrust and slow down the healing process.

Just like Otis and the police officers in the fictional town of Mayberry, the relationship between law enforcement and the community will work better when the officials that serve and protect have some sort of interest in that place, be it due to family living there or they grew up in the community and know the residents.

When this relationship is absent and little has been done to foster good relationships, the police may simply be viewed as an occupying force with no compassion for the people that they are supposed to serve.

Heredity vs. Environment

One of the greatest discussions ever known to man is the age old debate: "What has the most effect on a person's intelligence? Is it their heredity or is it their environment?" When this question was first posed to me in middle school, I answered that a person's environment has a larger effect on not only their intelligence, but their outcome as well.

Environment plays a very important part in how you perceive the world around you and how you will interact with it. Let's do a hypothetical experiment. What do you think would happen if you separated a set of twins at birth? You place one in a great home, sent it to the finest schools and gave it a stable environment. You probably would think that this twin would turn out alright, but not necessarily so. There are other factors that need to be taken into account when trying to determine what influences that person's choices. I'm sure we can all think of someone that we felt had it made and they just blew their opportunities.

Let's look at the other side of this scenario, say the other twin was placed in an unstable home where the child had no idea where or when the next meal was coming from and he/she had to move to a new home often because of ever-changing circumstances. You might possibly think that this person would be screwed up because of this. However, because of the way they grew up, this person made a commitment to make their life better and took advantage of every opportunity that was given to them.

When it comes to destiny, I believe it really boils down to the decisions that we make based on the opportunities we are given. What will you do with the opportunities that you are presented with?

Even though we are not animals, (or at least we would like to think we are not) I will use the example of a dog. Pit Bulls are often vilified by people because of the vicious way that they have been known to attack and kill. Even though that is a byproduct of what that dog can be, what usually plays a major part of the dog's outcome is the environment that it is raised in.

If you remember the TV show, *The Little Rascals*, Pete was a Pit Bull and he interacted with the children of the show as if he was one of the gang. Although there were several dogs used to play the role of Pete, there is no evidence that the American Pit Bulls used were ever taken off set due to negative interaction with the cast members. This, in theory, proves the age-old saying, bad owners usually result in bad dogs.

I recall when my children were young; we owned a guard dog. When my children were between the ages of one and four, that is my youngest child was one and my oldest child was four, we had a Bouvier. This Bouvier was one of the sweetest, meanest dogs that I have ever owned; but she was professionally trained in guard attack and obedience and never once harmed any of my children. The key there is proper training.

After she died, I was given a Rottweiler. For some reason, people are always trying to give me dogs and telling me that they think that I would be a great owner. (Yeah, right!) Anyway, I digress. My friend gave me this dog because he said that he wanted to make sure that it had a good home. I took the dog and began to train it as well. During the training process I was told by my uncle, "Make sure that you don't leave your dog outside because someone may try to steal him." My uncle said that Rottweilers don't begin to mentally mature until they reach the age of two. I heard, listened to and followed my uncle's advice; however I forgot to pass that little nugget of wisdom on to my children and guess what? Someone left the dog outside, unguarded; and he was taken. Who would have thought that you would need a guard to guard your guard dog? At the time, the dog had grown to be very large and had a really mean disposition.

Maybe I should have explained to my then oversized puppy: your bark is loud and your size is menacing, but you are not a guard dog yet.

Here comes the not so ironic twist of fate in this story. My neighbor saw the puppy being taken and told me the entire story as soon as I got home.

He said, "I saw the kids go up to your gate. I thought that they were coming to play with your kids; therefore I didn't think anything of it."

I searched all over the neighborhood for my stolen puppy and just as I was about to lose hope, a tip came my way from my friend who actually sold me the dog. This friend had moved a few blocks over from where I stayed and was informed by one of his neighbors that he saw some kids with a couple of Rottweilers. My friend then thought about it for a moment and considered that one of the puppies could possibly be mine. The neighbor of my friend also interjected his thoughts as to how he believed the children had taken him away. The neighbor stated that he believed the children brought a female dog up to the gate to lure my male dog away from home. Can you believe that a male was distracted by the a lure of a female? It happens more than you think, and not just to dogs of the animal persuasion.

Back to the story. I called one of my friends on the police force and explained to him my situation. My friend and his partner were working in my precinct. I asked him if they could come with me to see if this person had my dog. He said that they would be there right after they picked up some doughnuts. (Just kidding!) He came by; and we went to the person's house that we were told may have our puppy. When we arrived at the residence, we knocked on the door. The lady inside answered with a scowl, "WHO IS IT?"

My friend said, "It's the police," at which time he asked for the person by name that we were told took the dog. The lady that answered the door then asked was the boy in trouble and if so, what did he do?

I said, "I'm looking for my dog."

The lady said the boy wasn't home at the time but he did bring a dog home the other day and it was in the basement. "You all can go down there and check but I'm not going down there with you because that dog is mean and crazy," she exclaimed.

I said, "Yeah, that sounds like my dog. Where is he?"

As we began to descend into the basement, my friend said to me, "Man this better be your dog because if it's not, then it's not going to be pretty."

I said, "Don't worry. I have a crazy noise that I make that my dog responds to and if I don't get the right response, then it's a no-go." I made the noise. I heard my dog begin to respond the way that he always did when I called him in that manner. I opened the door and he jumped all over me and began urinating in excitement all over the place. Now that's what I call a successful hostage rescue. This goes back to what I touch on in the previous chapter regarding the keys to a better existence. The relationship that I had with these officers helped me to achieve my desired outcome.

The story doesn't end there, because like anyone that's been in a hostile captive situation, my dog had some post-traumatic stress. We had later found out that those group of kids stole dogs and used them for fighting. This manifested itself one morning when we were getting the kids ready for school. Like I mentioned before, every dog that I have ever had was trained and had a good temperament. However, after being held captive and initiated into dog fighting, my once well-mannered dog's temperament had changed. My youngest son was walking in the hallway and tapping two pencils together when my dog saw him doing this he began to growl at him. I don't know what he associated that action with, but I brought it to an abrupt halt. I caught my dog by the neck gave him the alpha male stare with some well selected verbal coaching; and we had no further problems with him, after I reminded him that he would be doggy stew if he harmed anyone in this pack.

Needless to say there had to be a complete series of retraining and reprogramming of my dog to ensure that he would not turn his aggression on anyone in the household. I was successful in doing this; and my dog Omen lived on.

I included this in this chapter, because I feel that having dogs in my home for protection kept me from having to deal with a whole lot of nonsense that was taking place around me. My dog trainer once told me that there are two things that burglars are afraid of: one is the click of a shot gun and the other is the approaching of a good guard dog.

There you have it, an example of how the change of environment can change how a person or animal reacts to the world around it.

Heredity is just as important. It plays a big part of what you are physically and how you cope with certain things. Depending on who you ask, some people believe that particular ethnic groups excel at academics or athletics, while other groups may not. I don't believe that to be true, because the learning of new skills requires a commitment from whomever is trying to master said skill. Therefore, be it academics or a sports playbook, you still have to make a commitment and be dedicated to the learning process. Part of what I'm saying is that people decide to commit themselves to a cause, because there is usually some sort of benefit to doing so. For the athlete, that drive may stem from the hope of earning a good living and being recognized as one of the best at what you do. For the academic, their drive may stem from the same objectives. However, they may feel that athletically, they may not be able to reach some physical achievement goals. And the same could be said for the academic. Either way, both must commit to their goal in order to achieve the level of success that they are seeking.

Heredity is not like horse breeding; you just can't put two smart people together and think that they will create a genius. The same could be said for horse breeding; you can't just breed two winning horses and expect them to produce winning offspring. If this was true for horse breeding, we would have had more Triple Crown winners by now. The same holds true for people. Think of the greatest athlete or academic of your era. If heredity was such a determining factor, wouldn't you think that all of the great people throughout world history would have had equally gifted children just like them?

Are You Tough Enough?

This is the question that you should be asking yourself when you face many of your life challenges. Being tough enough will be a major contributor with the success of you achieving your desired outcomes.

I want to share with you some personal frustrations that I have experienced by either choosing to root for someone who was not tough or not being tough enough myself.

Since I am a big sports fan, let's start here. Being from Detroit, I grew up as a fan of my local sports teams. One team in particular has frustrated me to no end. The team is the Detroit Lions. I no longer invest my emotions in this team, because they have a long history of failure. But their play-off run that ended in January 2015, did it for me. It was at that time I realized that the reason that this team has never won in my lifetime is that they weren't tough enough.

Let me give you a history of what I'm talking about. I will start in 1983. The Lions were 9-7 and played the San Francisco 49ers in the playoffs. Our kicker was steady Eddie Murray who rarely missed kicks inside of fifty yards, and had a chance to win the game with seconds left on the clock. Earlier in the game, he made a 54 yard field goal; and with 11 seconds left in the game, he was faced with a 43 yard field goal to win the game. I don't need to tell you what happened, do I? He missed what would have been considered a chip shot for him. (Mental toughness)

The year was 1991, and the Lions played in the NFC championship game versus the Washington Redskins, who, by the way, had crushed them earlier in the season 45-0. Facing the Redskins again, the outcome was the same. At the time the Redskins had an offensive line nicknamed The "Hogs" and a tough as nails running back named John Riggins. The Redskins imposed their will on my poor Lions and sent them home with their tails tucked between their legs. And you know why? Because in this case they weren't physically tough enough. (Physical toughness)

There were other equally disappointing losses that occurred during the 90s which lead to one of the greatest running backs in the history of the NFL to say, "I'm retiring." Barry Sanders was one of the greatest, talented running backs of all times. He walked away from football while he was still great at what he did. This made many people upset including myself. I never questioned his toughness because he proved that week after week running behind an offensive line that often didn't provide him the adequate running lanes that many of his peers on more successful teams were enjoying.

After giving it some careful thought, I said, *He's the smartest Lion of them all because he probably realized that it's crazy to do the same things for the same organization over and over again thinking that he would get a different result.* It wasn't happening for him then and it's still not happening.

As for the 2014 version of the Lions that made the playoffs, I now feel just like Barry. I'm done. As I watched the 2014 version of the Lions, all that I was looking for was one thing; to make a tough play when they needed to, so that me and many other fans could remove the label "same old Lions."

Needless to say, you know what happened by now because they are the Lions, just like we thought that they were and hoped that they wouldn't be.

As I stated earlier the Lions 2014 season ended in a playoff defeat in January 2015.

Here is what happened when the Lions lost the game. Many people felt that it was a blown call by the refs. But I refuse to use that as reasoning. The reason why they lost is because they were not tough enough mentally or physically. In spite of the bad call, there were still numerous opportunities to seal away the game and impose their will. Missed opportunities turned into excuses. Missed opportunities such as bad punts allowed the opposing team to get back in the game. It's funny how things that are not right get overlooked when you get your desired outcome; but those same things get magnified when you don't receive the results that you were looking for.

People ask me, "Why don't you just find another team to root for?" My answer to that is, "To me it's like going to a little league game and rooting for someone else's kid because your kid is no good."

I think we all get a greater sense of enjoyment if we are rooting for our own, be it a team or anything else. I find no enjoyment hitching my support to another team just because they have a winning history. To me that's too easy, because you can always switch to a front runner if your team isn't getting you your desired outcome.

When I look at the rest of my hometown teams and how they became winners one thing is quite apparent: they didn't win until they became tough.

One of my favorite basketball teams is the Detroit Pistons from the Bad Boys era. Many people outside of the city of Detroit don't care for the team known as the Bad Boys. Why? Because they say that they were a dirty team. However, if you take a step back and look at the big picture, the Detroit Pistons became a bi-product of the type of basketball that was being played during that era of the NBA.

During the Pistons maturation process, they would always come up short of winning a championship. They were often out manned and pushed around by their opponents. However the Pistons had one of the toughest players of his era and any other era since, and that was Isaiah Thomas. Isaiah Thomas is a six-foot-one-inch tough man from the south side of Chicago, also a tough area.

Once Isaiah Thomas infused his tough mentality into the team, along with the mastery of coach Chuck Daly, the Pistons stopped being a laughing stock and now became a force to be reckoned with. All this because they became tough mentally and physically. Along the way they had to learn toughness from teams like the Boston Celtics, who were not only a great winning organization, but also had a collection of some of the toughest players in the league at the time.

Many people outside of Detroit still don't like how the Pistons ascended to the championship level. But their teams were very willing to pick up Detroit players once they left the team. Hmm, I wonder why? Was it because they were still great players? Or were they looking to add a little toughness to their teams?

Toughness goes way beyond sports. If you are going to get your desired outcomes, you will more than likely have to demonstrate a measure of toughness.

Many of us would not be where we are today if not for someone else's toughness. When you look at the history of man, every ethnic group has had to overcome some sort of obstacle to ensure that they were not overcome by the circumstances of their time period. It's no different today. What is standing in your way and are you tough enough to overcome it?

Building Good Relationships

Something that goes a long way in the building of good relationships is communication and understanding. Communication is where the point of view or the vision of a relationship begin to take shape. This can be done through the expressions of your expectations and how you see things from your point of view.

Point of view is very important when trying to reach an understanding in the building of a good relationship. Point of view is just what it says, your view from the point in which you are located. Let's look at it a different way. Say two people worked in the same office and on the same floor for 10 years. One of the employees worked from a corner office with a wonderful view of the city. The other employee's office was located next to an elevator. The employee with the office that had the nice view always spoke of how great it was to work on that floor, while the person whose office was near the elevator constantly complained that the office was much too noisy and disruptive. Both of them experienced different points of view based on their location and proximity.

Here's another example of what I mean. Several children live in a home with one bathroom. Three of them slept on the same floor as the bathroom, while the others slept on the lower lever of the home. All of the children were awakened at the same time and given the same opportunities to prepare for school. Now the children that were on the same floor as the bathroom were able to get to it first and were therefore able to get washed up sooner, while those who had to climb the steps and wait to get in the bathroom to prepare for the day may or may not have gotten a breakfast that was hot. It's safe to assume that each set of children, based on their experience, may give a different answer if asked the question, "Isn't it great to live in such a nice home?"

That's why it's important to understand a person's point of view because it gives you an insight to how their thoughts and actions were shaped.

Know-How

Know-how can be a life saver. I don't know if many people in this world realize this; but you pay in life for what you don't know. Did you ever watch the television series, *Tarzan*? In the legend of Tarzan, a human baby was rescued from an airplane crash and raised by apes.

During his life, Tarzan learned the things that it took to survive living in the jungle. Years later, Tarzan was brought to the concrete jungle of modern civilization; and, although Tarzan had the know how to thrive in his jungle environment, this new environment was proving to be challenging to him because he lacked the know how to thrive from day to day.

Many of us are like Tarzan when it comes to our daily life. We lack the know-how to thrive in our surroundings which often causes us to settle for less. Every day we use things or do things without really having a working knowledge of what it takes to truly make that thing operate. Your car would be one of those things. Most people know that you need oil, gas and water for the engine to work correctly unless you drive an electric car; but if that vehicle begins to have issues or breaks down the majority of people don't have the know-how and lack the knowledge needed to get that vehicle operating again and back on the road. This is where you pay for what you don't know; for had you possessed the knowledge needed to make your car work again, you would not be paying someone else to do it. I'm not talking about the instances where special tools or equipment are needed; I'm referring to basic car knowledge.

Another example of us not having the know-how that we think we possess is when it comes to processing and growing the food that we consume. I think it's safe to say everyone knows how to go to their local market place and select the food and items that they would like to include in their meals. Well suppose you were the last person on earth, would you know what it would take to continue to live and thrive? We know how to consume food; but many people don't know how to grow food and process their food under the right conditions. We know how to eat steak, chicken and other foods; but if you had to cultivate them from scratch, would you know how to do it? The answer for many, including myself, is no.

As you go through life, you should be trying to get as much know-how as you can in an effort to create the outcomes that you desire. We are just like computers. What I mean by that is that we are powerful tools with almost limitless possibilities; however, we are only as good as the programming that is downloaded into us and our ability to access that data and put it to a useful purpose.

As I think about the many computers and electronic devices that I have owned over time, I realize just how underserved I was because I did not know how to access the full potential of that device. There have been times when I have gotten rid of or replaced a piece of equipment with newer and more up to date piece of equipment, only to find out that the previous device had the same capabilities. I just didn't know that the item I replaced had the same features. I just didn't know how to access them.

Our lives could be looked at in the same way. We have a desire to do certain things in our lives and some of us never do them because we lack the knowledge that we need to accomplish a certain goal or feat. Have you ever been in a situation where you had a desire to do something but you just were not sure how to get your desired outcome? I can think of many instance where I may have wanted to repair or build an item, but just lacked the know-how. The lack of know-how has slowed me down, or stopped me from completing many process.

I'm sure that we all know someone who has taken on the task of starting a business. This person may have had a great idea, but did not get their desired result. They either lacked the know-how to get what they were trying to achieve, or didn't have an understanding of what should be done to make the business successful. In times like these, my suggestion is that you should seek wise counsel. In other words, find someone who knows what to do and learn from them.

My personal experience is this. I never have written a book before. So in my effort to make my first book experience as successful as possible, I teamed up with someone who had more know-how than me. Christine Kloser and her team has helped me to tap into my skill set as a writer and author. Thanks, Christine Kloser and team!

Bullying

Bully: A person habitually cruel to others who are weaker.

Bullying is something that I think we all have gone through at some point in our lives. My own personal experiences with bullying helped to shape me in part to become the person that I am today. Bullying occurs in different forms from verbal to physical. In my case, I was verbally bullied by a classmates through name calling. I've been called things such as four eyes, raggedy mouth, peanut head, the list goes on and on. Every bullying situation is different; therefore I think that there is no one answer or solution to solving them.

One of the ways that I overcame my bullies was that I became great at capping when called names. What is a capping you ask? Capping is when you reply to a joke made against you with a better and much wittier response.

Keep this in mind: most of the time when people are bullying you, it's to cover up a deficiency within themselves that they don't want the world to know about. I said before that there is no one way to solve your bullying problems.

I want to share with you how my DAD became my life-long hero. I told you earlier that most of my bullying came in the form of verbal abuse. However, I recall one day when I was in the 8th grade. I was picked on by a guy who was a gang member. We were at recess. My friend and I were playing a game of paper football, in which you slide the paper triangle from one end of the table to the other in an effort to get one of the ends over the edge of the table without it sliding off. You get four tries to do this. If you are successful in the four tries, the other person puts his thumbs together and points his fingers up in the shape of a goal post.

After I had successfully completed my turn, I had to kick my extra point. When I thumped the paper through my friend's fingers, I hit it so hard that it flew over his shoulder and hit the guy that was a gang member.

When I hit him, I immediately apologized; however that was not good enough for him. He took off his hat and I knew that I was going to have to fight him. Here is where it became tricky. I knew I could beat this guy in a fight; however I also knew that if I did beat him, I was going to have to fight a whole lot of other people after school. We started to fight and as he came at me, I used the Mohamed Ali rope-a-dope tactic, since I was truly fighting a dope. As we were going at it, I stumbled over a chair while stepping back and fell to the ground. At the time that I fell, the teacher returned to the classroom and broke up the fight.

After recess was over, one of my friends told me I should probably go home because the guy was going to probably try to fight me again after school and have more people with him. I took my friend's advice and went home. When I got home, lo and behold who greeted me at the door, none other than my DAD, Luther Middleton, who just happened to be working afternoons that week. (Uh Oh)

Here is how the conversation went.

Dad: "What are you doing home so early?"

Me: "I got into a fight at school today."

Dad: "What I tell you about fighting?"

Me: "I wasn't doing anything. I was playing with my friend and I hit a boy with a piece of paper and he started fighting me."

Dad: "Da What?" (That's what he said. That's my father's word.)

Dad: "I'm taking you back to school right now. We're going to find out what happened."

Me: "No, daddy. Don't worry about it."

Dad: "What do you mean don't worry about it? Somebody is going to fight you just because you hit them with some paper. We're going to see the principal."

Me: "No, daddy. He's in a gang and he's got a gun."

Dad: "I don't care. Put your coat back on and let's go."

When we arrived at the school, we went to the office and they summoned the guy that I had the fight with. The first thing that my father said was, "Look at him he think he's one of those gangsters wearing that big old hat." The principal asked us what happened. The other guy said that I hit him with a piece of paper, didn't apologize, and that is why he fought me. My father asked me to show him what I hit him with. I made the paper triangle and showed it to him. My father asked the guy, "You mean this little piece of paper hurt you so much that you felt that you had to fight my son?"

I'm thinking in my mind, *Oh boy, I am going to be fighting every day for the rest of the school year or until this person is out of my life.*

But to my surprise, the other guy changed his tone when asked if the paper hurt him. He replied to my father, "No, Sir."

My father went on to ask him, "What is this that my son is telling me about you getting a gang to beat him up?"

He replied, "No, Sir. I ain't in no gang and nobody is going to bother your son."

My father then says, "Okay, so we won't be having any more problems?"

"No, sir," was the guy's reply.

"Now Donald, apologize and when you go to school you go to learn, not play games!" was my father's reply.

I'm thinking in my mind, *But it was recess and playing is allowed.*

Later in that school year, that guy and I were assigned to the same homeroom. I still always avoided him because he was just bad news. But one day, I do recall while sitting with a bunch of classmates, him coming over and talking to one of our mutual friends. He asked my friend, "Hey, you know my man right there?" referring to me.

My friend says, "Don, yeah I know him. He's real cool."

The guy says to him, "Yeah I remember him. We got into a fight a while back, and you know what? He fought me back, but we're cool now." The guy from the gang was shocked that I would even fight him back. I guess he was accustomed to terrorizing people without much resistance.

I know that my father's intervention and the actions he took that day helped me bring a bullying situation to an end.

Thanks, Dad. MY HERO!

While some bullying is physical and easy to recognize, bullying can also occur quietly and covertly, through gossip or on a smart phone or the internet, causing emotional damage.

As a starting point, there are elements that are included in most definitions of bullying. Although definitions vary from source to source, most agree that an act is defined as bullying when:

- The behavior hurts, humiliates, or harms another person physically or emotionally.
- Those targeted by the behavior have difficulty stopping the action directed at them, and struggle to defend themselves.
- There is also a real or perceived "imbalance of power," which is described as when the student with the bullying behavior has more "power," either physically, socially, or emotionally, such as a higher social status, or is physically larger or emotionally intimidating.

Many definitions also include:

- **The types of bullying:** The behavior can be overt and direct, with physical behaviors such as fighting, hitting or name calling; or it can be covert, with emotional-social interactions such as gossiping or leaving someone out on purpose. Bullying can also happen in-person, online or through smart phones and texts.

- **Intent of the part of the student with bullying behavior:** It is intentional, meaning the act is done willfully, knowingly, and with deliberation to hurt or harm, but there is some controversy with this statement, as some assert that not all bullying behavior is done with intent or that the individual bullying realizes that their behavior is hurting another individual.

- **Distinction about amount and duration:** Many definitions indicate that the bullying is "repeated," but the reality is that bullying can be circumstantial or chronic. It might be the result of a single situation, such as being the new student at school, or it might be behavior that has been directed at the individual for a long period of time.

- **The implications for all students:** It is also important to note that bullying is not just about the implications for those targeted by the behaviors, but that the behavior can impact all students in the school, including those who witness the behavior and those that engage in the behavior.

- **Additional factors:** These can include: the differentiation between bullying and harassment; enumeration of protected classes; statements around the use of technology; how the behavior impacts educational performance and the physical locations that would fall under the jurisdiction of school sanctions.

Students often describe bullying as when, "someone makes you feel less about who you are as a person."

Bullying may also be considered harassment when it is based on a student's race, color, national origin, sex, or disability.

Harassing behaviors may include:

- Unwelcome conduct such as: Verbal abuse, name-calling, epithets, slurs
- Graphic or written statements
- Threats
- Physical assault
- Other conduct that may be physically threatening, harmful, or humiliating

As I said before, every bullying situation is not the same and you may not know what the outcome might be; but here is some advice for those of you that are being bullied. "Don't keep it a secret. Let someone know. Find your hero. There is help out there for you. SEEK IT!!!"

Chapter IV

The Importance of Choosing the Right Mate/Partner

This topic is near and dear to me for a number of reasons. First of all, I may be biased when it comes to discussing this topic, due to the fact that I have been happily married for over thirty years now. I personally feel that being married or in a partnership with the right person enhances your life. It's a well-known fact that humans are social creatures and, more often than not, seek the company of others. Also, there are statistics that show that people who are married or in a long term relationship tend to live longer. And since I'm trying to live as long as I physically can, a loving marriage seems to be a good choice for me.

Keep in mind the relationship that you get into or the partner that you choose may not be seen by some as right for you. But remember at the end of the day it's your happiness and well-being that you are seeking not someone else's. People will always try to be the judge of how you live or who you choose, when in fact they may need some guidance and understanding of their own circumstances. My criteria for people and their relationship is if no physical or mental abuse is taking place and if you're not breaking any laws, then you're good. Every relationship has different mechanisms that hold them together and make them work. Therefore what is successful in one relationship may not be acceptable or work in another relationship. That is why there is a need for communication and understanding before you proceed in your relationship.

The Secret to a Long-Term Relationship

The question that my wife and I often get asked is the question you probably asked yourself when you read that I'm happily married and have been so for thirty years. And the question is, "What's the secret to staying married?" Well honestly, this information alone is worth the price of this book, no matter how much you paid for it. A person could write a long drawn-out book about ways to keep your marriage strong and long-lasting and all that good stuff; but in reality there is only one real answer to that question. Drum roll please! "The secret to staying happily married for a long time or remaining in any long-term relationship is: BEING ABLE TO PUT UP WITH THE OTHER PERSON'S STUFF." I use the word stuff only because this is a family-oriented discussion. But feel free to insert the word that you feel is appropriate.

You may think that isn't something nice to say for a man who claims to be happily married for over thirty years. Well, just to let you know, this has nothing to do with being nice; it has to do with being truthful and that's my truth. At any time, if you were to ask my wife, she'd actually say, "I took my marriage vows very seriously. I thought long and hard about for better or for worse and considered what I thought the worst could be." Then she'd roll her eyes and tell you the same thing I said, while laughing through the answer.

People get the meaning of happy and being in a happy state of mind confused all the time! I'm happily married because I know that happiness is a state of mind; and as long as my mind sees things for what they truly are, I am happy. Now, trust me when I say that during the entire marriage, I've not been totally happy or even had a happy state of mind everyday. But overall, and day to day, I am happy.

When you're in any type of relationship for an extended period of time, you'll have bad times, good times and great times. My good and great days have by far outweighed my bad days; and it is for that reason that I have been happily married for over thirty years. I am happy with my state of being and the person that I chose to live the rest of my life with.

I like being in a relationship with one person to buying a car. I use this analogy because I absolutely love cars and I think it fits well when describing people and long-term relationships. This is what I mean by that: when we buy a new car, if it's truly the car of our choice and it has every option that we want, we are totally in love with that car. We drive it, wash it, get oil changes every 3,000 miles and take good care of the car. A year or so goes by and we then realize that next year's model has a feature on it that we wanted in our first car. Not only does it have that feature, it's a more efficient model. You can consider trading it in to get the newer model or be happy with what you have and keep the car you purchased, because you've become attached to it. Now since people are unlike cars, we can't just switch them out every time we see what we think is a newer and better models. (Although some people do) That's why we need to make the right choice the first time we do it.

Things don't always work out this way. That's why there is such a high divorce rate. Economically, people can be financially devastated by divorce for what is termed the "switching cost involved with it." For those of you who don't know what switching costs are, it is the fee that you are charged to go from one business entity to another. Let me try to put it in a way that most people understand. When you are with a cell phone provider, and before your contract term is up, you decide that you no longer want to be a part of their company; you are usually hit with a fee to break that contract. This is what is known as a switching cost. The same applies in the instance of some marriages, when there are large amounts of assets to be divided one of the parties or both parties are hit with what amounts to a switching cost. This sometimes causes people to remain in relationships that are not good for any of the parties involved, children included. For this reason, you should adhere to what I started out talking about in this book, which is MIND YOUR BUSINESS.

By minding your business early in a relationship, it may help you to avoid some of the pit falls that are usually encountered once the relationship ends. Keep this in mind: whenever the time comes that you or the other party see fit to discontinue your relationship, always try to end it in a positive manner.

Friend of the Court

I was speaking with one of my friends recently, and I told him that I was writing a book. He asked me, "What is the book about?" I went on to tell him what I was covering in each chapter. He then said, "Man, that sounds like it's going to be pretty good. Don't forget to write about baby mama drama." I asked him, "Why?" At which time he went on to tell me how he didn't mind his business as it relates to making his child support payments. When he went to the court house to see what he owed, he found out that he was sixty thousand dollars in debt, related to back child support payments.

I told him, "Don't you know that the friend of the court is no friend of yours?"

He retorted, "Man, I know now, because my daughters are grown and I'm still making payments and I'm almost fifty."

I reminded my friend it wasn't baby mama drama that landed him in the situation that he found himself in. It was due to the fact that he didn't protect his brand and mind his business. The easiest way for many people to determine why they may be experiencing an outcome that they don't desire is by placing the blame on someone else. However, if we are honest with ourselves we can usually find the responsible party reflected in the mirror. If you are not all of the blame, you've more than likely played a significant part in where you are now.

With this in mind, we must also realize that being with the wrong person for whatever the reason can have a negative and long-lasting impact on us. Staying in a bad partnership can lead you down the pathway of bad outcomes, such as loss of sanity, money, and, in severe cases, your life.

Make the right choice, and if it turns out over time that it was the wrong choice, come up with an exit strategy that will preserve your business as you move on to the next phase of your life.

The Eyeball Test

The "Eyeball Test" is when you only give something a simple look over while trying to determine if that something is or isn't good for you.

The "Eyeball Test" may be good for short-term relationships; but, after all is said and done, there had better be something there more than looks keeping the two of you together. As the old saying goes, "Looks are deceiving." I'm sure that you can remember buying something based on looks; but when you got it home and went to use it, you were very disappointed and wanted your money back. When choosing the person you want to be with, it's not always that simple. You may be seeking a return that may not exist within your relationship structure or expectations. At this point, you need to be especially careful if you are choosing a person to spend your time with or possibly the rest of your life.

Men and women both fall victim to the "Eyeball Test," but I think that women get damaged by it more than men for this one simple reason: physical beauty, in some people's eyes, lasts only a moment.

Looks and so-called beauty have a shelf life; for women this is often exploited and the women are used and discarded after someone has made a determination that they don't have "it" anymore, whatever that "it" may be.

Lots of women's "brands" have been damaged by choosing to be with someone who did not have their best interest in mind. Here is a scenario that people can relate to. Guy meets girl. They have a relationship, and from that relationship a child is conceived. Guy leaves girl to raise child on her own, and the girl's brand is changed forever.

The reason that I say that the "Eyeball Test" damages women more is because, now that this woman has had a child, her body may have changed, and she may be more physically and mentally exhausted. These slight changes have also made the woman's brand change. She has to now market herself differently when she goes out to meet new suitors. Remember, she may have once described herself as a single woman or a single professional: but now she may have to refer to herself as a single mother, which may, in fact, turn off some potential partners.

During the time that a woman is trying to determine who is right for her, she needs to always remember to protect her brand, in an effort to keep the wrong person from derailing her goals and dream. Don't forget, protection, protection, protection! Oh yeah and did I mention, Protection!!!

This goes back, once again, to minding your business. If you're not building, leading and protecting your business, then who is? Don't forget when you become a part of the wrong kind of partnership or merger, your brand takes a hit. This is especially true if you are left to raise a child by yourself. Once you have a child or children, there will certainly be days when your child becomes ill and there is no one other than you to care for them. This may cost you lost time at work and income related to that lost time.

Here is why I think that the "Eyeball Test" has less impact on men in contrast to women. Most women will overlook the test if a man can fulfill an additional need or desire. For example: a man can be the oldest, ugliest and least attractive person that you have ever seen; but if he has financial status, the "Eyeball Test" is null and void. This hardly works in reverse, because of the standards that most men use when choosing a partner.

The Tie That Binds You

I remember saying earlier, that the secret to staying together is being able to put up with the other person's stuff. That's really only a part of it, even though that's a real important part. There is something else you need to consider. What in your relationship will help to hold you together when things don't go right? In other words, what is the tie that you have with the other person that will hold you together?

In my case, it was the love and care that my wife showed my mother doing one of my mother's most difficult times. If you recalled earlier, I mentioned that I am a U.S Army Veteran. I cut my military career short, because my mother was home by herself raising my nephew. One day while I was in Germany, my sister called me and told me that my mother had been robbed coming home from work. This really bothered me because I 1, knew that the neighborhood in which I had grown up in was now changing for the worse; and 2, I was too far away to protect the person who had loved and protected me all of my life. Neighborhoods are like people. They are always changing and evolving, but not always for the better. What makes a neighborhood is the people.

With this in mind, I decided to cut my military career short. When I returned home, my wife and our three children went to stay with my mother. During this time we began to notice changes in my mother's behavior. After going to the doctor for some tests, the diagnosis was that my mother had early onset Alzheimer's disease. My mother was only sixty years old at the time. The disease began to wipe away my mother's memory, just like a computer virus does to a hard drive. My mother began to forget who we were; and she would always call me by her brother's name, which was cool because I knew that she and her brother were very close. The day that it all fell apart for me is when I walked up to my mother and she asked me, "Who are you?" I went to my room and began to cry uncontrollably. As I write this story now, I am crying as if it was that day.

This story is about the tie that binds me to my wife. On the day I spoke of above, my wife came in the room and asked, "Baby, what's wrong with you?" I told her what had happened and she said, "Don't worry. We will take care of Momma." With that said, my wife and all of my family set aside any differences and gave my mother some of the best care that any person could get. I recall my wife taking care of my mother just like she was one of her children. She would feed, dress, bathe, and take her everywhere she would go. I saw the love and care my wife bestowed to my mother and that tie bound us from my end. You know, come to think of it, it takes a special person, to care for a mother-in-law or any other person that has health concerns. Sometimes you can't get a mother-in-law and a daughter-in-law to even share the same room without some sort of tension or find a good nurse or caregiver to come to your aid in your time of need. One thing is for sure, working in the healthcare field has given me a great appreciation of good health and good healthcare, neither of which are guaranteed as we go along our life journey. But I have also realized to that nurses are too often underpaid and underappreciated. So for all of the great nurses that I have had the privilege to work with, and for those that I have not worked with as well, I want you to know that I appreciate all of your hard work. (Salute)

There were some funny stories that happened on the way to discovering that something wasn't right with Mom. Here is a quick one. One day my mother was watching the children; now mind you, we had no clue that my mother was losing her cognitive abilities. My aunt called me and said, "Your mother is here with the kids." I then asked, "How did she get there?" My aunt said, "She walked from your house." That wasn't uncommon because, as I mentioned before, my mother and her brother were very close; and she would often walk to his house. What made this strange was my mother took the kids because my wife had left them in her care. This included my youngest who was wearing a "Onesie" at the time, a one piece pajama outfit. When I arrived at my uncle and aunt's home the children were fine, except for the fact that my mother forgot to put shoes on the littlest one and he walked a hole into the bottom of his PJ's. Grandma had taken them to the store before they embarked on their journey. I think the treats that grandma had brought along for the trip may have eased some of the concerns that children have when they are traveling, such as "Are we there yet?"

There you have it, the tie that binds. If you ask my wife it may be something else. I always ask her why do you love me? I'm not rich. I'm not a pretty boy. I'm not anything like those other boyfriends that you used to have. She says, "You're absolutely right about that, honey! And it is for that reason that you are my husband. A good man is hard to find; but an endearing man who loves his mother, his children, and his family is even harder to find. That's why you were and are my husband."

One more thing about my mate and the mate that you may choose for yourself: you may love the person that you love and no one may understand why. Guess what? You don't need them to understand; all they need to know is that you are receiving the things that you want from your mate and your relationship. At the end of the day, you should be able to say that I am better off being in a relationship with the person that I have chosen to be with. If you can't say that, then maybe it's time to re-evaluate. Don't forget: just like when shopping for anything new, just because you switch, doesn't mean that this will be the right one either. Remember there is always going to be some MESS.

Chapter V

The Importance of Maintaining Your Family Structure

Another critical point that I always tried to get across to my kids is that there is nothing more important to live or die for than your family. This topic is near and dear to my heart because I understand the impact of a fractured family structure. For the descendants of American slaves, more commonly called African Americans, this has been a long- standing issue that goes back to the American slave trade.

I am going to speak from my perspective regarding family structure. I will use the neighborhood that I grew up in for my example. The neighborhood that I grew up in was a very stable working class neighborhood. There were a total of 30 houses on my block, 15 on each side. Out of those thirty homes, 25 of them had children that lived within them. Those homes also had either a married couple within them or a mother and father present. As time passed, this began to change and so did the neighborhood. The neighborhood went from being a working class neighborhood in which people owned their homes and went to work every day, to a neighborhood that was made up of renters and more single parent homes.

As the family structure changed, so did the way in which people interacted with one another. When fathers were present in the home, there seemed to be more stability and less conflicts. During my youth, the men of the neighborhood were the protectors and the peacekeepers in the area. They watched over the younger generation of kids. This took place starting at the top with the fathers in the home, all the way down to the older brothers in the house. Real fathers and real men played an essential role in the protection and stability of a community. When they are absent, a large measure of order is lost.

I remember the day that my father died. At the time I was only 14 years old, and his death altered my entire family's way of life. The good thing was that my father left us well taken care of, because of his planning and the way he had structured his life. The bad thing about it was I lost a great inspiration and teacher. To the point of family, the men in my neighborhood watched over me and nurtured me through one of the toughest times in my young life. I grew up in a home as the youngest of six kids, five girls and me the lone boy. That is why I always stayed close to and tried to go everywhere with my dad. Although there was no one that could take his place in my heart, there were many wonderful men that stepped in to try to fill the void. For that, I am eternally thankful to those men. They have helped shape me and guide me through a tough portion of my life. That's what real family does.

Family is very important in the shaping of our life. Many people have more than one family. There is the family that we are born into and the family that we choose through relationships that they form later in life. Our birth family is where we get many of our early values and the know-how needed to navigate through our daily circumstances. Based on how receptive we are to our early teachings, we make a choice to do one or two things. We either stick with what we have been taught early on and build on it, or we decide to go in a different direction that is either slightly different from how we were raised or something totally opposite to our early teachings.

Our birth family usually is where we can find the most love, forgiveness and acceptance, more so than we can get from people outside of our family. When a person feels like they don't identify with their birth family, they might choose to disassociate themselves from their family and form new relationships with people who they have more in common with. This choice may be made based on a pursuit of happiness or personal survival.

The thing that makes family important to our overall success and happiness is the support that we receive from our family during the good and bad times in our lives. Without family, things become a lot more challenging depending on what you are trying to accomplish. As the saying goes, "No man is an island." I understand that many people feel as though they don't need anyone to get the things done. But I also know that many things become less difficult with the support of a good family.

The African American Perspective

As many people know, Africans were taken from their native land and dispersed throughout Europe and the Americas. This has had a long-lasting and devastating effect on the descendants of those people, since they rarely had a true sense of belonging and family. The American slave trade has a well-documented history of families being broken up and sold off for business reasons; it's no wonder that African Americans have struggled with the concept of family living. This was not and is not always true; but it just seems to happen too often.

People want to judge African Americans for the circumstances in which they live or for the day to day decisions that they make; but many fail to understand the actions that took place to land them where they are. I hear people say how they or their ancestors came to America with nothing and they pulled themselves up by their boot straps and made a good living for themselves and their families. What those same people fail to include with that statement is that they more than likely had some sort of support system.

One day, my college instructor explained to the class, "Everything is a system!" After giving it some thought, he is absolutely right. Everything that we operate on or within is based on some sort of system. Think about it We live within a solar system. Our human bodies consists of several systems: a respiratory system, circulatory system, a digestive system, etc. When we get in trouble we find ourselves in the criminal justice system.

Many systems were and are still designed in an effort to keep certain segments of the population in check. You may not want to honestly believe this to be true, but it happens to most people every day. It doesn't matter your age, race or gender. You are the subject of some kind of system of control.

Women find themselves entangled in a system that does not pay them equal to men; people who work in certain corporate jobs are sometime subject to a system that doesn't allow them to ascend past a particular level. I can go on and on about the systems that are in place; but I won't. Just remember, systems are put in place to control or keep things in a certain order.

Perspective

If you want to be fair-minded while trying to judge others, you must first try to take a walk in their shoes, or at least see things from their perspective. Remember I said earlier that two people can live in the same place, but can have a different perspectives based on their experiences. Imagine being home one day and someone comes into your house and kidnaps you. After being taken to a place that you know nothing about, you are forced to assimilate to the customs of your new living conditions.

During this period of being held in captivity, you have had no contact with your family and don't know any of the people who have held you captive. As time progresses, you form new relationships with your captors. You form families and have children and try to make the best of your captive state.

However, during your time in captivity, you see your loved ones being hanged, raped and sold away, breaking up the new family bonds that you have created. It would be hard for anyone to say that this would not have an effect on how they behave. Even now we see recent cases of people who have been kidnapped and returned home or military personnel that have been held captive. The effects captivity are long-term and devastating. Therefore it stands to reason that, if certain individuals need therapy when they are removed from a captive state, then why not others as well?

If anyone can go through all of that and say that it won't have any long- term effects on them, then I am going to have to respectfully disagree. Ask any parent today who has a missing child and they will tell you the effect is life-changing, not only for the parent who doesn't know where their child is, but also for the child who has been taken away and put into unfamiliar circumstances with strange people.

Perspective is when and where we determine if an issue is worthy of our attention or efforts. It would serve us all well if we took the time to see things from other people's perspectives.

Dad's Responsibility

Throughout my childhood I was taught that the man is supposed to be the head of the household. With that title came certain responsibilities, such as the care and protection of your family. Now I'm getting ready to go down a tricky and slippery road. I want to ask men this: How can you manage your responsibility when you are not around? You can try to get someone else to manage your responsibility for you, if you just can't be there. But remember, no one can do it like you can.

This is a question for men who get women pregnant and don't share in the responsibility of raising that child. Once again I want to ask you to put yourself in the position of a woman. A woman is impregnated by a man and goes through many physical and emotional changes of childbirth. She then gets left with all of the responsibility of raising a child that she made with someone else. Right, wrong or indifferent, this is the circumstance that many women find themselves in.

Let's look at it from a couple of different ways. Our human body is comprised of many different parts and organs. So, look at it from the standpoint where there are two parts such as eyes, ears, legs and arms. When any of these body parts are lost, it makes our way of life more challenging and then we have to seek out ways to compensate for that loss. You could say the same thing when referring to parenting; it takes the sperm of a man and the egg of a woman to bring forth new life in a natural way. After this is done, both parties need to maintain their roles to help ensure that this new life has the best possible chance to grow and thrive.

Dad The Protector

That is only the beginning of the process. What remains is a lifelong commitment that needs to be undertaken by BOTH parents. I understand that not every couple that conceives a child will live happily ever after; but every child deserves to have the love and commitment of both parents. When you lose the power of two, you lose a lot of the leverage that comes along with it. Even in the animal kingdom the power of two is more of the rule rather than the exception.

I have always liked to watch shows about animals in the wild. I have observed the pecking order or structures of many different animal groups. For example, the lion, the so called king of the jungle, actually gets much of the support of the pride (which is the equivalent to a human family) from the females of the group. The females do most of the hunting and all of the raising of the cubs. The main function of the male lion is the protection of the pride. And, oh yes, he gets to eat first after the ladies bring down the kill. Imagine what happens to the pride if the male is not there to protect it; the outcome is usually not good. What usually happens is another male comes along and kills all of the cubs and starts a new family of his own.

Since we are supposed to be smarter than animals in the wild, (debatable) then why can't we seem to get it, that in order to protect our family and ensure the growth of our offspring that we need to be there for them. Now that's not to say that every man who gets every woman pregnant needs to marry her because we all know how complicated that could get in many cases. But each person does need to be an active participant in the growth and development of their child.

When the protector is involved and doing what he is supposed to do, it limits the number of things that can go wrong. Like the example that I laid out earlier, when describing how my father got me out of what would have been a difficult bullying situation. I'm not sure if I had to navigate that situation alone that I would have made the right decisions, nor would I have wanted to expose my mother to that situation.

Any good protector will always use physical measures as a last resort because he or she knows that there is much more to be lost when a rational well thought out solution is not reached. That's why it's very important that the protector is there to fulfill his role. Could you imagine how many young ladies could be protected from the ill intent of people that mean them no good? I grew up in a home with five sisters. I can remember when my sisters would bring over male company, how my father would just so happen to need something from the kitchen. He would walk past the living room where my sister would be sitting with her company and go "UMM UMM." That was code for it's time for him to go. Parents have the ability to see things in young people's friends that they cannot see for themselves. It's a good idea to listen to them because they, more than likely, have come across some of the particular traits that they see and don't like about the person you are dealing with.

I was talking to a friend of mine the other day and we were discussing our dads. My father was always in my life and he died when I was 14. My friend's father was always in his life and his dad died at the age of 54 from a heart attack and at the time my friend was 25. We were talking about how much we really missed our fathers and how our lives would be different if they were still here. My friend said something profound to me and that was, "I wish I could spend ten minutes with my father right now, so that he could help me with some of the things I'm going through."

Think about how powerful that is. He's saying all he needs is ten minutes of his father's guidance and wisdom and he feels that he would be a better man for it.

Think of how it effects any child when their father is not there for them. Males need their dad's guidance, wisdom and perspective. Females also need his guidance and wisdom, but most of all his protection. If you don't spend the time with your children, you need to understand that you have still impacted their outcomes, only time will determine in what way.

Mom, The First Protector

If you take time and give it careful thought, you will realize that our mother provided us with the first and most important protection needed for us to be born as healthy as possible. Based on the choices that our mother's made it determined whether or not we would be exposed to things that could be potentially harmful to us. A good mother will sacrifice her own wants and desirers to insure that the child she is carrying is safe and protected from harm. It is this kind of selflessness that has endeared our mother to us for the entirety of our lives. Even after we are grown adults our mother's love and protection are there for us and help us navigate through difficult times in our life.

Mom The Teacher

Our mother is the first and best teacher that we will ever have. The connection that we share with our mothers is very strong because of the physical bond that we once shared inside of her. The critical parts of our development from the time of conception came from the nourishment and care given to us by our mothers, based on how she treated herself. For example, if she stressed; we stressed. If she smoked; we smoked. If she lived a healthy life, so did we. If she was at peace, so were we. These are some of the early stages of learning that we go through based on the experiences that we gather from our mothers. Since this is more true than not, mothers have to be very particular about what they expose their children to. All of the know-how that we obtained in the early stages of life is given to us by our mother, if she is the one that raised us. For the sake of this point, we will look at the events from the stand point of a biological mother raising her biological child.

Mothers teach us all of the things that we need to know in the beginning just to remain safe and care for ourselves on a limited bases. Like many cubs or offspring in the wild, we stay close to our mothers for protection and survival skills. Good mothers always sacrifice themselves for the well-being of their little ones. I always find it very surprising when a mother puts her children at risk of danger in any form or fashion.

Mother's Strength

I say this from a biased point of view, as I said before, that I grew up in a home with strong female presence. It is my belief that women are stronger than men in many areas, except for physical strength. I'm not saying this to butter women up or to make them feel good. I'm saying this because that's my truth based on what I have witnessed in my lifetime.

Women deal with circumstances that men don't have to deal with as much, such as the baring of children, getting paid less to do the same work as men. Furthermore, women are many times left with the responsibility of raising a family after things go wrong in relationships. Be it right or wrong, this is the reality for many of the mothers of this time.

Let's look at how a mother's strength helps us to develop into who we are. I said before that women are as strong as men in almost everything other than physical strength. That is debatable as well, since there aren't many men that I know of who would be willing to change places with a woman when it comes to childbearing. The women who I know tell me it is one of the most physically draining, but most gratifying times of their life. I can't imagine spending hours in labor. (Ouch) A mother's strength usually goes well beyond the physical once she is blessed with the responsibility of a new life. Mothers sometimes are faced with the tough choice of do I eat or does my child eat?

I recall watching Kevin Durant making his speech for the NBA's MVP award. He gave high praise to his mother and the sacrifice that she made to ensure that he and his siblings had the food they needed to eat. I don't think that there was a dry eye in the house, including mine. This is what good mothers always do, give more of themselves than you may think is possible at the time. I bet each and every one of us could fill many pages of a book if we shared how our mother's love and strength got us through tough times or protected us from dangers that we weren't aware of. The great thing about this is mothers do this from the time we are born until the time that she can do it no more. For those men who think of themselves as self-made and feel that it's a man's world, keep in mind you wouldn't be who you are if it wasn't for a good mother's touch.

Message from Dad to Daughter

For all of the moms and potential moms, if I could share one thing with you as it relates to maintaining your family structure, it would be this: "Protect your brand." Remember what I said earlier, "You are a business!" How you build and protect your brand will go a long way in helping you reach your desired outcomes. Careful thought must always be done when you are considering who you will be having relationships with and how far you will go with them. If you are not trying to be a mother, then make sure that you take the proper steps to protect yourself from that happening.

People are who they are and rarely do they change. Don't go into a relationship thinking that you are going to change a person from what they really are. They may disguise themselves for a little while; but if you observe them long enough, they will show you who they really are and what they are all about.

Don't have a child in hopes of making a man stay with you; there is historical evidence that shows that this is a flawed strategy. If a person wants to be with you, they will do so because of how they feel about you, not because you're pregnant. Remember, when you give birth to a child, you are changing your brand. You are going from a sole proprietor to a partnership to a multiple business entity. Make sure that is what you truly want at the time, because it changes your brand forever.

Who is in Your Family?

My sister used to always say to me, "You can choose your friends, but you can't choose your family." This is true when it comes to our biological family. She would say that to me because I would always tell my sisters that they were all crazy. And I do mean that literally. The statement that my sister used about not being able to choose your family is partly true. I say this because most of us have people that we consider family, only after we grew to know and love them over the course of our life.

The people who we choose to be in our family says a lot about us. Take for instance people who run away from home and join gangs or other such affiliations. This is usually done because of a feeling of disconnect with the people whom they have been around all of their lives. A person usually takes this path when they feel the need to be a part of something that they are not getting from their current conditions.

Since I grew up in a home where I was the only boy, I chose who I wanted to be my brothers. The good thing about that is you can assemble people of your liking to help you meet the wants, desires and needs that you have. The friends I have, that later became like brothers to me, come from all walks of life. What society deems as a good person or a bad person was not the determining factor for whether or not I would deal with a particular individual. What determined that was the love and respect that they showed me and my family.

My closest friend, the only person who knows the ins and outs of me better than my wife became addicted to drugs. We grew up together as neighbors from the time that we were babies; he lived two doors down from me. He was almost like my live-in brother, as he was one of the only guys that my father would let roam freely though the house.

We both joined the Army together, but we didn't serve at the same duty stations. Sometime during his enlistment period, my best friend got hooked on drugs. When he returned home, his parents were devastated. I saw him do many things that I thought he would never do. I saw him steal from his parents, take his father's car and pawn it for drugs and other unmentionable things.

One day he had returned home from one of his long drug binges. I asked him, "Man, where have you been? Your wife and parents were worried sick about you and why didn't you call me?"

He told me, "Donald, I love you and your family too much to let you see me like that. You are a good man and your kids are like my nieces and nephews; and I don't want them to see me that way. I'm embarrassed." That's a powerful statement of love coming from someone who loses themselves due to the powerful effects of drugs.

As with all relationships, family, friend or foe, you must always know where to draw the line. Knowing where to draw the line will keep you out of places that you probably have no business. As I stated before, I have friends from many walks of life that have told me, "I'm getting ready to go do something you can't do because I don't want you to be involved. You're a good dude and I don't want anything to happen to you." They also knew where I draw the line regarding certain matters. (Much respect)

It still comes down to the family structure and whether yours has been naturally created or formed through your choosing or design. You do better as a person when you are a part of a good one.

Chapter VI

The Importance of Good Negotiation Skills

From the time you are born until the time that you die, you are negotiating. Here is one of the truest and critical parts regarding negotiation and that is: "You get in life what you negotiate." This is true whether you feel that you are actively participating in the negotiation process or are silent.

We start our negotiation process beginning in our childhood; when a baby is crying, it is actively engaging in the negotiation process. As the child begins to grow and develop, it adjusts its negotiation tactics based on the response that he or she receives from its environment.

As we begin to get older, we learn to verbally communicate our desires; this then triggers another change in our negotiation practices. I bet we all can remember negotiating with our parents to get a little more time to stay outside and play with our friends.

Parents and children are always in some form of negotiation, be it passive or authoritative. Can you remember being told that your allowance would be withheld or your privileges would be denied if you did not do what was required of you? Well, that is a form of negotiation. One party is communicating their wants and desires while the other party is trying to determine how to get the most out of the negotiation without giving up too much.

As a child, our negotiation position isn't very strong, since we were relying on our parents for the majority of our support and really had very little to offer as a counter measure. Even though most children have limited leverage during negotiation, many make the most of their skills, in an effort to come out as winners. When we start school, there is another level of negotiation that is reached, as we encounter new people and form new relationships. Our teachers are usually the next party that we find ourselves locked in negotiation with.

Here are some of the scenarios that cause us to enter into negotiation with our teachers. Late homework: usually after forgetting to turn in our homework, we seek some form of extension from our teacher. This is done by trying to build a case for getting an extension on the predetermined deadline. Another scenario would be, after being a distraction in class, you are told to leave. For the sake of your principal or parents not finding out about your impending disciplinary action, you enter into negotiation with your teacher to give you one more chance.

Don't forget we are always negotiating. Even when we're deciding who we are going to date and why we are going to date them, a level of negotiation takes place. This is done to determine whether the person is a right fit for us at this time in our life.

Dating and marriage relationships would go much smoother if the negotiation is done before the relationship starts rather than at the end. Think about it. Guy meets girl, girl gets mad at guy or vice versa. They are mad because one party may feel the other party spends too much time with their mother. This then causes a rift in the relationship because the other party feels that they are not getting the attention that they deserve. However, this probably all could have been avoided if they both had communicated prior to getting into a committed relationship and laid out their wants and desires.

For example the conversation could have been as simple as this: "Honey, I want you to know that I usually spend Sundays with my mom. I go over and check on her and she cooks a big dinner for me and the rest of the family. Do you think that this will be a problem for you if we are together?" Simple questions such as that can possibly open up the dialogue needed for many other important conversations. Conversations are always good starting points in most matters.

The next major negotiation that we will find ourselves involved in is for a job and or salary. Like I stated before, when taking a job it should be a win-win situation. If you are not getting the benefits that you seek from the job that your taking, you won't be happy with your decision long-term.

I remember during my working career when I was given a promotion at one of my jobs. At the time, I was trying to determine how much I should ask for in salary. My wife told me to ask for five thousand dollars more than what I was going to request. After making the salary offer that I had come up with, I later felt that my wife was right. I should have asked for more money, because my boss at the time granted the request of my initial offer without any push back. What really made me disappointed about my lack of negotiation for my salary was the fact that I realized that I would always be getting five thousand dollar less that I should be getting annually. Be that right or wrong, I will never know because I was never allowed to go further in the negotiation process.

Car negotiation is one of the most tricky and deceptive negotiations that you will find yourself in. Most people walk away as a loser after the deal is done and don't even know it. Every day around the world, cars are sold to uninformed consumers. I never understood how two people could go to the same location and buy the same car and pay two different prices. Well I understand now; it's called negotiation. Good negotiation skills during the car-buying process can be the difference in you owning a car that you enjoy driving and that is within your budget, or waking up kicking yourself every morning because of buyer's remorse.

The same is true when buying or renting your first home, since the terms and conditions are usually negotiated by both parties. It is in your best interest to do as much research as possible, due to the fact that you will be entering into some sort of written long-term agreement.

Leverage

When you are entering into the negotiation process, it's best to gain as much leverage as you can in an effort to get your desired outcome. Have you ever heard someone ask, "How did he or she come away with that or how did that person get to keep their job? They must have had something on the other person."

This could be true or not true regarding a successful negotiation process. One thing is for sure the more leverage that you have during the negotiation process, the better chance you have to win your battle. Negotiation still requires a certain level of skill and know how. Remember, just because you have leverage, doesn't always mean that you will be successful.

Leverage can be misused or possibly even turned against you, depending on how the other party views what you see as your leverage or advantage. When it comes to the proper utilization of leverage, the timing of its use goes a long way in the success of its application. When you use leverage, it should not be something that is brought into play to destroy or do irreversible damage to the party that you are negotiating with. Keep in mind, the principle of fairness, seeking mutual benefit and maintaining a relationship are keys to a successful outcome.

Why Negotiate?

Negotiation is an inevitable part of your life if you intend to interact with other parties. Negotiation helps when conflicts and disagreements arise and parties have aims, wants and beliefs. Depending on the goals of the parties involved, the position that they are taking may result into an argument and resentment, which may lead the other party feeling dissatisfied. You should use negotiation in an effort to reach agreements without causing future barriers to communication.

Many wars are avoided between differing countries because of the negotiation process. However, war is sometimes the last result of failed negotiation. When the war is brought to a close, there is still some sort of negotiation that takes place, which makes most of us say, "Why didn't the parties at odds with each other just do that in the first place?"

Negotiation has varying stages that you will need to use in the effort of achieving your desired outcome. The stages are as follows:

1. **Preparation:** This is when you need to gather all of the pertinent facts about the situation that you are embarking on. This will be used to help you clarify your position. Preparing yourself before entering into your negotiation will go a long way in avoiding conflict and unnecessarily wasting time while negotiating.

2. **Discussion:** This step is where you and the other party or parties make your case from your point of view or as you see it.

3. **Clarifying your goals:** This step is when you and the other party lay out your interest and viewpoint. Prioritizing your goals is helpful, through this it is often possible to identify or establish some common ground. When you clarify your position, it can help you avoid misunderstandings that are likely to occur which may cause barriers to you reaching a successful outcome.

4. **Negotiate towards a win-win outcome:** This is where you and the other side come away feeling that you have achieved most or all of your goals. Although this may

not always be possible when negotiating, it should be the end goal that you are trying to achieve. Different strategies and compromises may need to be considered at this point. You can use compromise as a positive alternative in an effort to help you and the other party achieving a better result, as opposed to holding on to your original positions.

5. **Agreement:** Once both sides get to a level of understanding agreement can be achieved. At this point, everybody should keep an open mind so that you can achieve an acceptable solution. Agreements should be made very clear so that you and the other party know what has been decided.

6. **Implementing a course of action:** This is where all of your hard work yields you the objectives that you set out to accomplish from the beginning of the process. At this point you should be feeling some level of satisfaction knowing that your efforts have helped you to obtain some or all of what you set out to do.

Buying Power

When you master the negotiation process, you increase your buying power exponentially. Remember earlier we talked about the buying of a new car and depending on how your negotiation went determined whether you walked away happy or with buyer's remorse?

Buying power coupled with a well-thought-out negotiation strategy will save you countless money over time. One of the best strategies for you to use is preparation. When you are prepared it increases the options that you have at your disposal for getting the best deal.

Here is a scenario for you to consider. We always see car companies advertising what they consider great deals on their vehicles. For example, the ad may say, "Sign up today to get a great lease deal with zero down and zero out of pocket." You see this deal and run over to the dealership to pick up what you consider to be a great offer. However, when you arrive at the dealership you find that those terms aren't for everyone. The terms advertised are for people with a high credit score. Unfortunately many people who set out to get this deal do not have the credit score that is needed to get the advertised terms and conditions. Therefore they either take a lesser deal or leave without the new car that they dreamed of.

Preparation will go a long way with helping you achieve your desired outcomes. When you are making a major purchase such as a house or car, the strongest negotiation tool that you should take with you is your ability to walk away when you know that the deal is not to your liking. As bad as you may want to make a particular purchase, you should know and understand that the person who is selling the item wants you or someone else to have it just as much. The key here is reaching terms that are agreeable to you.

Listening goes a long way. If you take the time to listen to the other party, they will almost tell you everything that you need to win in your negotiation process. Why do you think that when you go in to buy a car, the salesman starts to ask you certain questions? At that time the salesman is feeling you out and trying to figure where they are going to direct you in your buying process. Remember at this point, your preparation will go a long way. If you are able to communicate your needs clearly, it keeps you on the path way that you have chosen for yourself and not the one someone is trying to take you down. So don't forget- listen, listen, listen. If you do this, you then give the seller a chance to reveal what they are trying to accomplish as it relates to meeting certain quotas or monthly goals.

I met a car salesman who told me that he averaged 12,000 dollars a month selling people extras during the car buying process. He said that is where some of the biggest profit is made, as it relates to the selling of extended warranties, protection packages and vehicle upgrades. He said these thing are usually sold to unprepared buyers or to people who have the money and aren't really concerned about the extra cost. Well if you are anything like me, you are concerned about the extra cost and would like to keep the money in your bank account if you can. So make sure you are prepared when entering the negotiation process.

    Negotiation is a skill that you need to master and refine daily to get your desired outcomes. A bad negotiation session is usually a by-product from lack of planning and preparation. So always go into a negotiation with a solid plan and an even better exit strategy so that you can come out feeling like a winner. Finally, when in a tense or heated negotiation, don't hesitate to use one of your most powerful leveraging tools if things aren't going the way that you like, that tool being the power to walk away, or hit the reset button.

Chapter VII

Choices
(Race/Religion/Politics)

This topic is near and dear to my heart, because I realize that everything that we are, have been or will be is determined by a choice. Outcomes don't end with the choice itself. What impacts the choice you have made the most are the actions you take after making your choice. Everything that you have done or will do begins with a thought. Your thoughts then manifest into some sort of action. That action, usually leads to an outcome. Inaction is also an action as well. It can be described as the action of doing nothing.

Whatever choice that you decide to make regarding race, religion and politics will be evolutionary and revolutionary as it relates to your life outcomes. Even if the choice that you make is to stand idly by and do nothing.

Race

One of the definitions of race as it relates to humans is: 1) a family, tribe, people, or nation of the same stock; 2) a group of individuals within a biological species able to breed together; 3) a category of humankind that share certain distinctive physical traits.

> **Racialism:** a theory that race determines human traits and capacities; *also* : racist

> **Racism:** a belief that some races by nature are superior to others; *also*: discrimination based on such a belief.

These definitions were taken from the Webster Dictionary.

As my children and I began talking about the topics of this chapter, I told them that they should be mindful of who they discuss them with, because not everyone is willing to have an open and honest dialogue about these sensitive topics. These three particular topics by themselves are a lightning rod that leads to very spirited debates and sometimes even bloodshed. It is for those reasons that I recommended to my children that they should always get their facts straight and be ready to support it with evidence.

Fortunately, I grew up in a home where as a child my parents didn't really shape my view of race based on their past experiences. Honestly, I can't even recall any conversations that we had about race. I can remember my mother always telling me that, "You are too rebellious" and, "When you rebel you don't hurt anyone but yourself." However, my rebellion was never directed at an individual or group because of their race, it was always in response to what I felt wasn't right. The treatment that I have received from people of all races, creeds and colors throughout my lifetime has been wonderful. I know that everyone can't say this, but that's my personal truth and I wish everyone could experience that. I have always had something in my spirit that told me to take action or speak up when something is not right.

I recall when I would go up to the University of Michigan to visit my sister on the weekends, her friends would call me the mini Middleton militant. I got this title for the way that I spoke out regarding things that I thought that were not right. I was only twelve at the time. I can remember catching the bus downtown after school to the Greyhound bus station and riding it up to Ann Arbor. Boy, the world has really changed a lot since that time! I wouldn't feel comfortable letting a twelve year old ride a bus downtown and certainly not take an hour ride anywhere alone now. As I said before, the world is very different. Also I have been very fortunate to have good people protect and watch over me.

As it relates to me and my racial experiences, I guess that I can say that my experiences have not been bad individually. I don't have a reason or a formula for that; it's just been my experience during my lifetime. Certainly when it comes to matters of race, things can always turn without warning. I am well aware of the systems and injustices that people face every day. But that's only part of the problem. The things that are put in place to oppress and destroy you can only work up to a certain point. You need to understand that it's you who may be giving your oppressor the additional power that they need to keep you in the condition that you don't want to be in.

In the example below, I will point out how this particular scenario could lead to different outcomes based on the actions that are taken. As I told you before, I have always been rebellious, but over time I have learned how to use my rebellious nature in resourceful ways.

I have always had my windows tinted on every car that I have owned. In Michigan, there is a law that restricts you from having your front windows tinted. I was pulled over by the police; and during the time of the traffic stop, I was informed that it was illegal to have your front window tinted. The officer told me the reason that the law was in place was because tinted front windows made it difficult for the officers to see your hands when they approach the vehicle.

The rebellious part of me was thinking internally, *That's a bunch of bull, because if I was in a van or a big truck you also couldn't see my hands as you approach my vehicle.* However, I kept those thoughts to myself and just listened to what the officer had to say.

Since I understood that while pulled over on the side of the road is no place to have a disagreement with the police, I decided to go to court and fight the ticket. In court, I learned that there was some exceptions that would allow me to have my front windows tinted. The judge said that the only way that I could keep my windows tinted is if I had a medical condition that was documented by my physician. The judge gave me thirty days to obtain the needed documentation. I obtained the documentation that was needed for my situation and the case was dismissed. Remember what I discussed in the previous chapter regarding negotiation. Some of those strategies were put in place in this example to help me achieve my desired outcome. I even recall being pulled over several times after getting my physician's letter. One day after presenting the police officer with my documentation, the officer read it, handed it back to me and said, "Man, that's a sweet letter! Have a nice day."

I used that particular example for these reasons. When the police reference the information contained on your license plate, they already have a pretty good idea of who you are and what your legal status might be at that time. However, statistics have shown that traffic stops involving people in the minority communities often lead to escalated and sometimes confrontational encounters that end in an unfortunate way for one party or the other and sometimes both.

I want to make a broader point by letting you know that race and culture and how they are viewed depend largely on where you are at any given time and who is in charge. For example, let's use the same scenario involving a traffic stop, but this time let's make it an international occurrence.

There have been many instances of Americans traveling abroad and being stopped by the law enforcement officials of the country that they were in at the time. Some of these stops ended in extortion or physical abuse from the law enforcement of the host country. Usually, there is no recourse for the victims that have been mistreated and it doesn't get reported. Which goes to show that racism and prejudice is often the tool of the people that are in power. In America, we see it as a black and white issue. However if you ever have the opportunity to travel around this wonderful world that we live in, you will find that people use race as a factor wherever they interact with one another.

My real message to you regarding these type of scenarios is to have your business in order and don't do anything that could make a potentially bad situation worse.

Since we are talking about race, I certainly understand that certain people in our society make a determination regarding me based on the way I look, where I come from or even the car that I drive. Speaking of that, during a particular time period, I drove a 1996 Chevrolet Impala as my daily vehicle. One day my vehicle broke down in a shopping center parking lot. As my wife and I were sitting there waiting for roadside assistance to arrive, my wife overheard a lady say to the person she was walking with, "Boy, that's a nice car. I bet you a black person or a Mexican owns it. They always spend all of their money on cars." Let me put this in perspective for you, this happened in November of 2014 when my car was eighteen years old. Funny, I didn't understand the relevance of the comment and I tried, for a moment, to determine if what she was trying to say was that I spent all of my money maintaining it or that I actually purchased a vehicle that I couldn't afford because of her perception of people of color. In the end it really didn't matter because I understood that those comments came from that person's point of view, which had no effect on my outcomes.

In another instance a woman stated to me, "That's a really nice car, but it looks like a drug dealer's car."

You should have seen the look on her face as I said to her, "Well, that's strange. I didn't know that drug dealers drove a particular type of car. That would make them kinda dumb to drive around in a vehicle that sends a message that says HEY I'M A DRUG DEALER!" I told her I bet that makes law enforcement's job so much easier. She replied, "I guess you're right about that. I apologize if I offended you." I said, "No need for apologizes. Have a nice day." My wife said to me, "You wanted to say something smart to her didn't you?" I told her, "I already did. That's why she apologized."

I have lost count of the number of times that I felt that I was being pulled over because of the car that I was driving. I can't place the blame on driving while black because remember, the only black the police see is on my car and on my windows. This only seems to happen when someone I know asks me, "Don't you get pulled over for having your windows tinted like that?"

At which time I reply, "No, but I am now because you asked me that question."

I usually get a good chuckle for some of the reasons that police have used to pull me over. Here are some of the good ones.

- Your vehicle fits the description of a vehicle that was used in a crime earlier today.
- When you made that left turn from the left turn lane, you didn't have on your signal.
- Your center light in your back window is out.
- Your trunk was open, do you mind me looking in it?

As I said before, I am well aware of the systems that exist and of the systems that don't have my best interest in mind. But what I am also aware of is that I have a say in the outcomes that I get. Out of the many instances that I described I would say that 95% of them turned out favorably because I protected my brand.

I tell my children, "Don't put yourself in a position where people can try to judge you based on how you look or act. Make them engage you in dialogue so that you both can get a better understanding of each other."

We know what the problems are, now let's work on some solutions to get your desired outcomes:

- **Self-Respect-** It's harder for someone to disrespect you when show respect for yourself. Don't forget whether you think that it is right or wrong. People do judge you by your appearance. So young men and women, when you choose to make a fashion statement remember you are sending a message about your brand. Whatever that message may be, you must be willing to live with the outcomes that it brings.

- **Honor your mother and father-** or whomever took the time and patience to help to get you this far in your life's journey. I recall one day getting into trouble as a teenager. I remembered the look on my mother's face and how it hurt me to see her that way. From that day on, I decided that I would never do anything that would cause my mother hurt or shame.

- **Take control of you narrative-** most stereotypes come from people who are telling your story the way they see it. Don't let someone control how people see you. Take control of your branding so that others can see what you are really about. One day during basic training, one of the guys in my platoon had said that he was from Buckeye, Arizona and where he lives, "There ain't no 'trigger word' there." Now if I have to tell you what the trigger word was then you need to get that education that we spoke of earlier. Let's just say the word rhymed with TRIGGER! After we reformatted him and gave him a course in brand recognition, he apologized. He explained that the only time he saw black people was on TV. He said, "I thought all of you walked around with boom boxes on your shoulders and were pimps and prostitutes." I was amazed at his ignorance. I say ignorance because he honestly didn't know anything different; and that was his reality. However, after getting to know us, he said, "You're nothing like I thought you were. Wait till I tell my mom." (I can't say it enough, TAKE CONTROL OF YOUR NARRATIVE.)

- **Make a determination of what will be your operating system-** In other words, establish and maintain your code of ethics. Once you do this you will have established a point where you draw the line. I was watching a movie one day, where a group of mercenaries were sent out to kill their target. When they found their target, that person just so happened to be with a child. One of the mercenaries was going to carry out the mission, but then the other mercenary said, "NO! Not with the kid there." The other guy said, "What difference does it make? We have a job to do." At which time mercenary one shot and killed mercenary two. Even though both of these men had the same assignment, one of them had a code of ethics or an operating system that drew the line at killing in the presence of children. (Where do you draw the line?)

- **Rebuild your family-** All of our families have their measure of dysfunction. But you know what? For every fool in our family, there is always one person that they look up to or respect. When you come across a fool find the person that the fool listens to and have them work together to strengthen family ties. This will go a long way in your effort to get your desired outcome.

- **Stop sabotaging your goals, dreams and ambitions-** I said earlier, that we usually need to go no further than our closest mirror to find out where all of our problems begin and end. Self-destructive behavior has led so many people and the people around them to a place that they don't want to be.

- **Don't wait for someone else to sit you down or take away your freedom, in order for you to gain perspective-** Take the time yourself to sit down in a quiet place, focus your thoughts and energy on what you want from your world and the people in it and then go out and create it. I've heard and seen too many times where young people get locked up and, while locked up, proclaim how they are going to change their lives when they get out. The reality of this matter is that the change they speak of rarely happens. In order to make a successful transition back into society, you need to have a good support system that you are willing to commit to. Most people don't have one or aren't willing to commit to the process that will give them the outcome that they desire. These matters usually lead them back to incarceration and a cycle of hopelessness and despair. Time is a precious commodity that you can't put a price on. Don't throw away any of your precious time on foolishness.

- **Learn how to forgive-** *Forgiving* allows you to grow in ways that you may have thought were not possible. *Forgiving* is the first stage of your healing process. *Forgiving* doesn't remove scars; but it helps you to deal with them in a positive way. *Forgiving* is not a sign of weakness. It's your proclamation that you want to continue to grow and get better. *Forgiving* doesn't mean that you have to forget what it was that took you to the place where forgiveness is needed.

Always remember this so that you won't repeat the past negative outcome.

- **Take care of where you live-** It's a proven fact that when people have dominion over something they tend to take better care of it. For example, when people rent cars or homes it stands to reason that they won't usually give that item the level of care that they would if they owned it.

- **Understand and realize that you don't own anything in this world not even your life force-** You may be thinking. What does he mean by that? What I am saying is that we don't actually own anything; we are simply the caretakers of whatever it is that we have in our possession or are seeking to obtain. For example, your life. You never knew when you were going to be born and you don't know when you are going to die. But, you do have a say in how your life progresses. This progression revolves around the kind of caretaker that you are. Do you smoke? Do you drink? Are you surrounding yourself with people that put you in harm's way? These are important matters that you need to give careful thought to as you move through your life's journey.

- **You don't own your offspring-** They are just under your care until they are able to become caretakers of their own lives. Even all of the material things that people acquire along their life's journey, they never own them. They are just under their care until they get passed on to the next caretaker. Homes are not owned. You may have the deed to the house but the government owns the property. If you don't believe me stop paying the taxes and you will find out who the real owner is.

- **Seek Peace-** One of the greatest gifts that any person can have in their life is PEACE! Peace often gets taken for granted; but you need to understand there is no greater gift than peace. There are people with a lots of cash resources, however they may not be able to enjoy them. That money doesn't bring them peace. Sometimes it's the way that they have obtained the money as well that causes them not to have peace. Things that you may take for granted such as walking through your neighborhood, sitting on your porch or enjoying an evening dinner with your loved ones may not be available for another person because of the existence of chaos and the lack of peace that surrounds them. Peace is one of the greatest gifts that you can give or receive.

Those are some of the starting points that you can address as you take control of things. Race is used as a divisive tool in an effort to keep good people from coming together and living in peace. When confronting the issue of race, if it was as simple as you looking at a person and saying that they are a particular way because of their race, then the evaluation of people would be an easy task. However, it is not that simple. Race, like other matters in your life, requires your engagement.

If a person could say, "My life is great because I live around people who are of my race and they won't harm me because we are all the same." Then you could make a strong case to that person that this is a delusional thought process and, as great as that would be if it were a reality, it is the farthest thing from the truth. The truth is that people are victims of crimes perpetrated against them mostly by the people within their own race or from within their community.

When acts of crime are reported on the news, it sometimes is categorized as black on black crime. By reporting the matter in this way, a hidden message is sent saying, "They are doing it to themselves." However at the end of the day, it's just simply a crime. When other races harm one another, it's not reported as white on white crime, Mexican on Mexican crime, or any other nationality that you want to insert here. IT'S JUST CRIME, PERIOD. Terms such as black on black are used to spark a certain response or emotion. When a person from another race kills someone else, it sparks a particular emotion. These emotions usually come from past experiences. Whether those feelings are justified or not justified, a person should be outraged by whomever is committing the crime.

Friends and Race

Any one of my children's friends that came by our house knew, if you were coming by to visit and there is work to be done by the family, you had better put on some work gloves. They also knew that they were going to have fun and eat good food. The funny thing is that kids always stayed and always came back. My kids' friends would always tell them how good they had it and that they wished that they could come and stay with us. It took some time for my children to realize that, but thankfully they finally did. Growing up they had friends from different nationalities and races, but at the end of the day I told them that they were just your friend, not your white friend or your Asian friend, just your friend.

Race and racism are learned behaviors. When two children come together and play, all they know is that they are having fun or not having fun with someone. If you never told these kids that they had things that made them different, they would go along and continue to interact without focusing on their differences. However, when someone else comes along and begins to point out their differences and or shares certain beliefs, then the friendship may change, depending on how this new information is received. Most people are smart enough to not let these tactics affect their relationship with those who may be different. However sadly enough, it only takes one negative force to spoil a good relationship. When those forces come your way, this is the time that you need to be strong and protect your relationship with your friend no matter what race they are.

Race in America

One day while watching the news, the topic of race in America came up. One of my children asked me, "Daddy, why do so many people dislike America and want to see it destroyed?"

I had to give this answer some careful thought, because I wanted to keep things in perspective and not sway my child's thinking one way or another.

This is the example that I chose:

Me: "We live in this house right?"

Child: "Yes"

Me: "Imagine someone coming to our door needing help in order to survive. We give them help, give them the know-how that they need to survive and help them through their tough time. After they learn how to survive, they then start doing harmful things to us, move us to a certain part of the house and take control of our home."

Child: "That's not fair."

Me: "We are not talking about fair; we are talking about why some people feel the way they do about America. I'm not finished yet. After taking your home from you, this person says to themselves, 'I got big plans for my new home. I'm going to start my home improvement project.' Now these same people who took your home from you, now go across town and grab a bunch of people off of the street, bring them back to your house and make them do the home improvement project. While doing this home improvement project, the workers are raped, beaten and killed. Oh and by the way, they were not paid either."

Child: "That's some BS. (Sorry, pops)"

Me: "I'm not finished yet. This same person who has obtained your home by questionable means, now tells the people who were here before them that they can't come back here because they are illegal and no longer welcomed here. That is just a small sample of why some people feel the way they do about America. I just used three different nationalities of people but there are more."

Child: "Do you think it will ever change for the better?"

Me: "Only when America is willing to deal openly and honestly about its history and the systems of racial hierarchy that it has in place. It has nothing to do with being fair. America is big business and always minds its business interest, you need to make sure that you do the same."

I could have gone on and on about race in America; but my objective was not to shape my child's thinking. It was simply to get him to think. I went on to further explain that race is an issue across the world. People from the same countries with the same heritage can still find themselves at odds because of race.

Race is a matter of perspective. Depending on their point of view, two different people can witness the same thing happen, but feel differently about it based on their perspective. When it comes to matters of race, if it was as simple as putting all like people together in an effort to gain harmony, then we could just go to that place and based on that premise everything would be fine. But it's not that simple, most racial matters involve a particular mindset that is being push by a person or a group of people. Change will occur when you transform the minds of the individual or group that is seeking to keep you where they want you to be. That will require diligence and hard work on your part, so you need to make sure you are prepared and tough enough for the task.

Religion

Religions of the world -- and individual denominations or traditions within these religions -- teach very different beliefs about the existence of God, Gods, the Goddess, pantheons of Gods and Goddesses, etc. They have very different views on the nature of deity, humanity, and the rest of the universe. But almost all share one belief: that they alone have the fullness of truth, and that every other religion in the world is wrong. Even within a single religion, many denominations, traditions and faith groups teach mutually exclusive beliefs, including the belief that they are right and all of the other faith groups within their religion are wrong -- at least to some degree.

Another tricky conversation that I had with my children revolved around religion. Once again I was not trying to shape their views. However, I wanted them to realize how important this choice is and how it could impact their life.

When trying to explain religion to my children, like always, I wanted to start out by defining what religion is by definition.

According to the Websters dictionary, religion is defined this way.

> **Religion** 1: the service and worship of God or the supernatural 2: devotion to a religious faith 3: a personal set or institutionalized set of religious beliefs, attitudes, and practices 4: a cause, principle, or belief, held to with faith and ardor. (source: The Merriam Webster Dictionary)
>
> **Religious** 1: relating or devoted to an acknowledged ultimate reality or deity 2: of or relating to religious beliefs or observances 3: scrupulously and conscientiously faithful 4: fervent, zealous. (source: The Merriam Webster Dictionary)

After defining what religion and religious is through a written source, I then had to go back and define some of the words that defined it and what they meant. While doing all of this, my message to my children was simply this: "Don't get religion and being religious confused with whether or not you think, believe or know that there is a God almighty." God is real and you need to always acknowledge that.

I explained to them that sometimes people try to dismiss, destroy or even avoid things that they can't understand or explain. I said the vast majority of people realize that there is a supreme being or force that controls us all; they just can't agree on how to honor it and pay their due respect.

I told them we are all spirits and we are born with a certain set of coding and within that coding is our connection to God. When a person does something wrong, most of the time they know it's wrong because of the feeling that they get while first thinking about it. As I said before, "Everything that we do begins with a thought." Then as a person acts out their thought, there still is a level of consciousness that tries to speak to their Spirit in an effort to guide them in the right direction.

I further explained even the people who say there is no God, seem to always call out for some kind of God to save them when they get in a bind. I asked my son, "What's the first thing people usually say when something out of the ordinary happens?"

My son replied, "Oh my God!"

I said, "Right. Now son, here is where it gets extra tricky. The God that they may be calling out to may not be the God that you are thinking of. People worship and feel a connection to God in many different ways. Many people are willing to die for their religious beliefs and even kill in the name of their God. But I want you to understand that God almighty doesn't need anyone to kill in His name, because the same way that we were activated into existence, God can very well deactivate us."

The thing that I wanted my children to understand is that they should always seek the spiritual wisdom of the Almighty and be willing and prepared to deal with the consequences that come with their choice. And so should you.

Politics

Politics 1. the art or science of government, of guiding or influencing government policy, or winning and holding control over a government 2. political affairs or business, especially competition between groups or individuals for power and leadership 3. political opinions. (source: The Merriam Webster Dictionary)

Politic 1. wise in promoting a policy < a ~ statesman> 2. shrewdly tactful. (source: The Merriam Webster Dictionary)

Political 1. of or relating to government or politics 2. involving or charged with acts against a government or political system. <~ prisoners> (source: The Merriam Webster Dictionary)

Politician : a person actively engaged in government or politics. (source: The Merriam Webster Dictionary)

When you get involved with politics you should enter the arena with the knowledge that you are about to enter some very murky waters, filled with slimy creatures that reside in dark and tricky places. That's why it should really be called "PILE OF TRICKS" instead of "Politics" because that is what many people get left with when they enter the political arena.

Transforming Your Political Landscape

In an effort to help you understand why you need to be involved in politics, I will cite some instances. When you are engaged in political conversations, you can move closer to your desired outcome.

Let's start with something as simple as voting. When we get outcomes that we weren't seeking in our day to day life, they can usually be traced back to the voting booth. Voting is often taken for granted in American culture; but if many of us took the time to realize the impact of who is elected into office, we would surely take the time that is needed to vote. On occasion, I have been as guilty as the next person when it comes to exercising my voting rights. I had, like many others, became disillusioned with what the voting process has yielded me. But after a wake-up call from my wife, who reminded me of the many people who had died just for us to get this right, I became re-energized and regained my purpose and focus.

That's what Politricks (politics) will do to you if you allow it to. Politrickcians will get you to focus on things that don't matter in an effort to confuses you while they advance their agenda.

Messaging

How you get your message across and who delivers it goes a long way, as it relates to getting your desired outcomes. Let's briefly discuss the tactics people use when they disagree and how they show their displeasure. When you are choosing the wording for your message, make sure that it is relative to the point and topic in which you are trying to convey. You should always make sure that you stay on message; and if outsiders seek to come in and bring harm to your cause or message, make sure the distractions are removed and continue to get the results that you seek in the manner that you choose.

The messenger is also important. You may not be the right person to deliver the message that needs to be heard. If this is the case, seek someone that can deliver your message effectively and with your goal in mind. Choosing the wrong messenger can take away from your objective. If someone tries to link you with a messenger that is not in line with your policy or practices, make it clear that they are not speaking for you and then take the control back of how your message is delivered.

Getting Your Desired Political Outcome

Getting your desired political outcome will take some heavy lifting that will require some coalitions and cooperation with others. In order to get political power you must be in possession of three key ingredients:

1. Money
2. Power
3. Access

Money can buy access and partners which will align you with your message and help influence others to forward your agenda.

Power is what you will need to put the change into action. Power can come in many forms; but the greatest power is the power of the collective people.

Access gets you to the place that you need to bring about the change that you are seeking.

Politics and political power are the things that keep many of us separated and not understanding how we are more alike than different.

A person can have money and still have no power. If you have power, you can get money. If there is a question of what to get first, get some power and the money shouldn't be far behind.

America was built on big business!

While mentoring young men in an after-school program, a young man asked me, "Why do people always say negative things about the way we dress?" I said, "That it is the nature of some individuals, to try to make you feel a particular way about your way of life and the choices that you have made." I went on to explain that people are willing to overlook your clothes, your attitude or whatever else they don't like about you when your business is successful and you have a measure of power.

When people come to America from different countries to do business, the focus is not on their attire. It's about closing the deal or coming to an agreement to achieve a desired outcome. So my message here is: get some economic power and that will be a good start towards the outcome you seek.

If you are seeking political power, having the right connections is a big help. If you have a prominent last name, you will probably have a much easier time running for political office because of the name recognition that your family name holds. Most people will have to start from the bottom and work their way up, as with any business. For politics, it could be something like running for student congress or student president in high school/college. Volunteer and campaign for political candidates that you support. Get the experience, because that's the first thing people will want to know. It will be helpful if you can get an internship. Make sure that you listen to people, be observant and learn as much as people are willing to share with you and more. A lot of politics seems to be public relations, therefore you need to be able to do just that. (Relate to the Public.) Write and speak well. The ability to articulate your thoughts in oral, as well as written form, will be essential to getting you into the right places and keeping you there.

Things that you can do to gain political power and influence

- **Know the Terrain.** You have to understand the terrain of your domain in order to defend it, or to take control of someone else's. In this modern world, mastery means understanding the use of voter databases.

- **Know Your Neighbors.** People are much more amenable to persuasion by people whom they already know, like, and trust. A deep and wide personal social network in your neighborhood is a priceless asset. In such an environment, the person who already knows the people behind those doors can recognize their faces and be recognized. Familiarity doesn't breed contempt - it breeds votes in this case.

- **Become a Trusted Information Source.** Just as folks are more amenable to persuasion by people they already know, they are more likely to believe and be moved by information from a source they already trust. Be a trustworthy source of information - and take that trust seriously by not abusing it - and you can move people and determine votes with the information you provide. Whether you are dropping off campaign literature on a regular basis, just chatting over the fence, or writing your own digital newsletter or blog, get people used to being able to rely on you for political information and half the work of persuasion is done. When you are the most politically informed and trustworthy person in your social networks, people will look to you to connect with the candidates and the issues for them. People aren't lazy when it comes to politics; they are efficient.

- **Deliver Seed Money and/or Political Contributions.** Having your own fundraising network of even small dollar contributors will quickly make you a sought-after political commodity. Those additional links in your political network will open new doors in your social landscape and give you further credibility as a political power broker in your locality.

- **Deliver Volunteers.** Money is wonderful; but, especially in local races, the real currency of power is people's time and effort. Most local campaigns rely heavily on volunteers to man the phones, canvass the neighborhoods, and keep the campaign moving. If local candidates can come to you and walk away with a pledge of volunteer staff, you become their most valued ally. Whether you provide this service through your formal networks, such as your union, service organization, church, or club, or by personal recruitment of your neighbors and friends, you will be a welcome guest at any political function; and people will always be sure to take your calls and answer your emails.

- **Get Elected.** Or at least try running for something. If you use even a few of the strategies outlined here, you will have people interested in you running for a leadership position; and rightly so, for you will in fact, be a leader. Whether it is a party leadership position, a stint on a board or committee, or public elective office, you can make those positions enhance your position as a local power broker. Don't run simply in order to run, and don't do it for the small amount of discretionary power the position may provide, that is the surest way to ruin the reputation you've built. Run to build your social network. Run to meet and form working relationships with people. And always run with an articulated and thoughtful goal firmly in mind - something that you can accomplish using the position you seek - and make that goal, your rallying cry.

- Lay out what you've accomplished in the past, the good qualities you bring to the table, the recommendations from your social network, and what you would like to accomplish for your constituents. It is vitally important that you make your goals clear in being elected or selected, that is the essence of a mandate; and having a clear mandate will make it easier to succeed in office. Even if you aren't successful being elected, you can only improve your reputation and name-recognition by playing the game fairly. That means no dirty tricks, no questionably ethical practices, and no lying about your plans once elected. By participating directly in the electoral grinder, you will have a better appreciation of the pressures on political candidates hoping to be elected.

Final Thoughts

If you have been entertained or enlightened by some of the stories that I have shared with you during this process, I'm humbled. However, I want to share one more thing with you and that is for you to be RESPONSIBLE with everything that you have been given authority over. You may be asking yourself what does he mean by that. Well, here is the answer. Along your journey through this life, you may be blessed to come together with another person and create a new life in the form of a baby. However, just because you have supplied one of the necessary components to create that new life, that doesn't make that child yours. What in fact makes the child yours is when you take RESPONSIBILITY for it and its well-being. The same goes for your own life, once you reach a certain point in your life's journey, it is your responsibility to make sure that you are doing the things that are needed to enhance your life and the world around you and not destroy it. Also, make sure that you are a good caretaker of the time that you are given from this day forward. Time is a precious commodity that slips away before you know it. Keep in mind that once time passes you can never go back and get a do-over; therefore, make sure that you are making the right choices at the right time, to help you achieve a life free of regret.

Congratulations!

You have completed one step in your journey of accessing your full potential. Every journey begins with a thought, but the actions that follow are the steps needed to make that thought a reality. It should be clear to you by now that reading this book is just one of the many steps needed to reach your desired outcome. The next step comes from the actions that you take toward your goal completion. This book provided some guidance and scenarios that will assist you as you face life's many challenges.

Don't forget that every journey starts with one step; take the steps that you need to get your desired outcomes. I'm sure that you have heard people use phrases such as, "I'm just killing time or I'm just doing this to pass the time." Time is the most precious possession that we get. Many people don't understand the value of time, until it is too late. You can't kill time; however over time, you will cease to exist. You can't pass time, however if you don't make the right choices at the right time; time will pass you by and you can't go back for a do-over. Therefore, throughout the rest of your existence make sure that you, "Use your time wisely."

I leave you in peace.

About The Author

Donald Middleton is fiercely committed to guiding and inspiring young men and women to achieve their full potential that allows them to build the life and business of their dreams.

He has been married for 32 years and is father of three children and four grandchildren. He is currently a manager in the medical field, and also does youth mentoring and speaking engagements.

A proud veteran of the United States Army, Donald enjoys learning, teaching, traveling, playing sports, home improvement projects and automotive restoration.

He is the founder of Fresh Start Consulting, an organization focused on helping individuals get their lives back on track after life-altering events. Donald's specialties include leadership, team building and organizational structure.

He has worked with several entities doing youth mentoring in the Detroit public schools. Donald has also given guest speeches at churches and community organizations.

To find out more about Donald, go to:
http://www.dadsconversations.com

www.ingramcontent.com/pod-product-compliance
Lightning Source LLC
Chambersburg PA
CBHW070628300426
44113CB00010B/1705